THIS IS MY SON

THIS IS MY SON

by

Don Churchman

DIANTHUS PUBLISHING

✝ *This is My Son*

Published by Dianthus Publishing
for the Intercontinental Church Society
175 Tower Bridge Road
London SE1 2AQ
Tel: 0171 407 0588

© Don Churchman 1995
ISBN 0-946604-08-8

To Ron and Pat
without whose practical help
and encouragement I would never
have put pen to paper

Foreword

There was much else that Jesus did; if it were written down in detail, I do not suppose the world itself would hold all the books that would be written.

St. John himself realised that the Gospel is an inexhaustible source of life, and as such would constantly lead believers into deeper and more wonderful understandings of the ways of God. In a sense the whole of the Bible is a reflection on the mistery that *the word became flesh, he lived among us, and we saw his glory.* St. John however has a particular way of taking us to the heart of the paradox of the eternal, timeless God making himself known through the words, things and gestures of our world.

The author of *This is My Son* is himself, if you pardon the pun, a devout and biblical Churchman who hopes that through these studies *many will come to know Christ as Saviour and Lord and that others who already believe will grow in the knowledge of him, whom to know is life indeed.*

There can be no greater aim for anything that we do than that, and as one occasion for the publication of this book is the recently celebrated 150th anniversary of the Diocese of Gibraltar (now *in Europe)* I am glad of the opportunity in this foreword to acknowledge with gratitude the contribution that Don Churchman and the Intercontinental Church Society have made and continue to make to the building and nourishment of faith.

✝John Gibraltar.

PREFACE

There is no way that I felt the need for yet another commentary on St.John's Gospel, still less that I should be the one to write it. A combination of factors, however, have encouraged me to offer the following studies in what I hope will be to many a new and refreshing approach to the fourth Gospel. The course does not follow the normal verse by verse method adopted by most commentators, nor do the chapters consist of 'sermon reproductions'. What I have done is to rearrange a series of lectures I have been giving on the Fourth Gospel to the student at Tauernhof Bible School in Schladming, Austria, for the past five years and reproduce them in such a way as to be useful for home Bible study groups.

Intercontinental Church Society, to whom I am grateful for undertaking the responsibility of getting this work into print, had suggested that such a book would make a fitting contribution to the 150th anniversary of the founding of the diocese of Europe. Also, in view of the 'Decade of Evangelism', the book should be evangelistic in essence. What could be better than a series of studies on St John's Gospel?

In my opening paragraph I have referred to a 'new' and refreshing approach. In what way could these studies be regarded as 'new'? I am sure there is nothing in the following chapters that has not been said before but I have yet to come across a book which seeks, in a sustained manner, to draw out how the writer of the Fourth Gospel fulfills his self-expressed purpose of persuading his readers of the truth about Jesus and receiving life in his name. 'These are written that you might believe that Jesus is the Christ, the Son of God, and that believing you might have life in his name' (John 20:31). The pressure of every chapter in the Gospel is to lead men into faith. It therefore becomes supremely evangelistic. Unless we grasp this central element, we shall never understand its deeper mysteries, let alone enter into the promises held out to the sincere believer.

I have avoided deep and controversial issues of a critical nature. It did not seem to me to be profitable for those involved in home Bible study groups to get bogged down, as they inevitably would, in the textual and philosophical obscurities which many find in this Gospel. Indeed, to do so would cut across our intention. There is a sense in which the Fourth Gospel is well within reach of the simplest mind and yet out of the reach of intellectualism. Such is the mystery of divine revelation. May I, however, refer those who feel the need to pursue this line of study to consider the works of Bishop Westcott, C.H.Dodd, C.K.Barrett, Wm.Hendriksen, R.V.G.Tasker and John Marsh, all of whom I have read to my great profit and who have stimulated my own thinking on the text of the Gospel. I have given some background to the studies in the Introduction and have set it out in such a way as to promote discussion. At the end of each chapter I have offered some questions which I trust will generate profitable interchange of thinking among group members.

My prayer is that through the pages of this book many will come to know Christ as Saviour and Lord and that others who already believe will grow in the knowledge of him whom to know is life indeed.

Don Churchman
January, 1995

CONTENTS

Contents

INTRODUCTION TO THE GOSPEL OF JOHN

All quotations throughout this commentary are taken from the New International Bible

When studying any book in the Bible it is essential, if we are to understand the intention of the writer, to consider who wrote it,when he wrote it and why. This must be fairly obvious to any serious minded student. If, for example, the Fourth Gospel was not written by St John but by some unknown person, the book would immediately lose its apostolic authority. This would mean that instead of sitting under its authoritative revelation (i.e. the divinely revealed truth concerning God and his purposes) the reader would sit above it, passing his own judgement upon the message. He would feel free to compare it with other writings as equals not giving it the unique status it deserves. It is this recognition of the divinely inspired nature of the apostolic writings that gives the Gospel its ultimate authority. Paul,writing as an apostle, says this 'We also thank God continually because, when you received the Word of God, which you heard from us, you accepted it not as the word of men, but as it actually is, the Word of God' (1These.2:13). As Paul further reminds us,'All Scripture is God-breathed' (2 Tim.3:16). It is helpful to remember that the criteria for inclusion in the New Testament Canon of Scripture was that all the evidence pointed to apostolic influence.

Establishing the date of the Gospel is equally important because it not only makes a valuable contribution in determining the authorship but also enables the student to determine what access the author had to other early Christian traditions. For example: were the synoptic Gospels already in circulation? If they were, did the writer of the Fourth Gospel make use of them?

Finally,confirming the intention of the author in writing the Gospel is essential in helping the student to interpret its message. There is no merit in concluding that 'this' is what you believe the book to be saying unless you have studied it against the background of the writer's aim.

1. WHO WROTE THE FOURTH GOSPEL?

It is a good starting point to mention that very few biblical scholars have challenged the traditional view that the Fourth Gospel was written by the man whose name it bears. It is not quite so straightforward in the case of some other books in the Bible, but as far as this Book is concerned, opposition to the view that John, the beloved disciple, is the author, is in no way formidable. To establish the identity of the author of any book requires that we look into two areas for our evidence: internal(what, if anything, the book itself has to say) and external(what history and other writers have to offer).

Internal Evidence

Bishop Westcott, Barrett and many others have written at great length on this and other related subjects, so I will simply draw your attention to certain passages and inferences that can be drawn from them. The author seems to have been a Jew with considerable insights into Jewish customs and beliefs. There are many references to the Old Testament, with which the writer is clearly well acquainted: e.g. the author makes the comment,'His disciples remembered that it is written, "Zeal for your house will consume me"' (2:17; see also 10:34-5; 12:38-41; 13:18; 17:12; 19:24-8,36-7). He seems to have a special awareness of the current understanding of Messiah who should come (1:41; 4:25; 6:15). He makes reference to no less that four major Jewish festivals: Passover (2:13), Purification (3:25), Tabernacles (7:2) and Dedication (10:22-3). That he may have been a Palestinian Jew is well emphasized by his apparent detailed knowledge of topography, especially the district around Jerusalem (1:28, 5:2, 9:7, 11:1, 18).

We can go much further than this and with a fair amount of certainty, conclude that the author was actually one of the disciples, if only on the basis of the detailed record of events,the intimacy of the conversations, and the conciseness of the discourses. References to this are numerous. Here are just a few: 1:29f.; 2:1-2; 3:24; 4:6, 40,50-3. Some readers will be able to add considerably to these passages.

One further piece of biblical evidence is found in the book of the Revelation and the epistles of John, which are never seriously doubted as being anything other than the work of the apostle John. There is a very strong likeness in both language and style between the Gospel and the books mentioned (e.g.,compare John 1:1-14 with 1John.1:1-10.

External Evidence.

Of the second century writers, the following are the most important to us in this respect. Clement of Alexandria wrote, 'John, urged by his friends and inspired by the Holy Spirit, composed a Gospel', whilst Irenaeus attributed the fourth Gospel to John the apostle. Origen, an early third-century writer and one of the greatest expositors of the Scriptures, said, 'John,the beloved disciple, wrote both the Fourth Gospel and the Apocalypse'.

We are, in fact, standing upon very firm ground when we say that to read the Fourth Gospel is to read words truly inspired by the Holy Spirit through the pen of John the disciple whom Jesus loved.

2. THE DATE OF THE GOSPEL.

Having confirmed that John the apostle wrote the Gospel, we can establish that it was written before AD 98 because we know that the was banished to the Isle of Patmos during the persecution of Christians under the Emperor Domitian AD 81-96. He returned to Ephesus at the beginning of the Emperor Trogan's reign, and died in AD 98. John clearly knew Mark's Gospel and actually made use of Matthew and Luke which must have been after AD 85, the date generally ascribed to Matthew. John's Gospel was therefore written soon after AD 90 and almost certainly on the Isle of Patmos. It was late enough to hold in focus all the apostolic traditions circulating at the time and early enough to be historically accurate.

3. THE PURPOSE OF THE GOSPEL.

This has already been hinted at in the preface, but we need to be a little more precise in our conclusions. There seem to be three main thrusts behind the Gospel.

To Supplement the Synoptic Gospels.

The synoptic Gospels, Matthew, Mark and Luke, are so called because they provide a synopsis of our Lord's life and ministry. John does not do this in the same way. He focuses on the person of Jesus and his message rather than on giving an historical account of events. We have seen that John had access to the earlier Gospels, but although he makes use of them he does not quote them extensively or reproduce common source material at length. We can note the following as instances of supplementation.

The synoptics all give an account of the baptism of Jesus. John does not. What he does is to use the occasion to herald the coming of Messiah, the Lamb of God who takes away the sin of the world and who will himself baptise with the Holy Spirit (John1:26-34). The synoptics give an account of the institution of the Last Supper. John does not, but he does record an amazing discourse on the Bread of Life (John.6). The synoptics recount the story of the rich young ruler who asked about eternal life. John does not, but he does unfold the doctrine of eternal life fully in chapter 7. It can be seen from these few examples that what, to some extent, is obscure in the synoptics is often given theological significance in the Fourth Gospel.

To Refute False Teaching

St John's Gospel has sometimes been referred to as an apologetic, that is, a defence of the Christian faith against heresies. Certainly Gnosticism was abroad at the time. Gnostics sought to combine Greek philosophy with the Christian message, teaching that evil was based in the flesh and was not of God, who was remote from the world. It can easily be seen how John attacked such teaching when he stated, 'the Word became flesh and lived for a while among us' (1:14). One of their foremost teachers was Cerinthus, with whom the apostle John is said to have had an encounter at Ephesus. Although this is by no means the main purpose of the Gospel, it was nevertheless written in an atmosphere of heresy and John loses no opportunity to refute it.

To Implement John 20:31

Here we come to the underlying purpose of the Gospel: 'These are written that you may believe that Jesus is the Christ, the Son of God, and that by believing you may have life in his Name.' Here we have three strands. 1) to expose Christ for who he was; 2) to elicit faith; 3) to promise life to those who believe in his name.

To Expose Christ for who he really was.

When John the Baptist heralded Christ with the words 'Look, the Lamb of God', he was in fact expressing the purpose of the Gospel, which is to reveal Christ to the world as Saviour, Messiah and Son of God. As we proceed we shall see that the author, above everything else, seeks to persuade his readers of the Saviourhood, Messiahship and deity of Jesus. He is the complete and only Saviour of lost mankind. He is the one whom the Old Testament prophets said would come and redeem Israel, and he is none other than God himself. Through his personality, Jesus reveals God's person and character; through his teaching he reveals God's ways; through his ministry he reveals God's power; and through his death he reveals God's love.

To Elicit Faith.

There are two words that constantly recur in John's writings:'believe' and 'receive'. Sometimes they are brought together, as in John.1:12, 'To all who received him, to those who believed in his name, he gave the right to become children of God'. Clearly, the one is meant to give emphasis to the other. We might say that to believe is to accept objectively what is revealed concerning Jesus, that he is the Saviour of the world,the Messiah, the Son of God. But devils also believe this because they know it to be true (James 2:19). So we may begin here, but there is a need to go further. To receive Christ is to go further by submitting to him in obedience and faith. In the Gospel, John is never satisfied with just an objective acceptance of truth. He calls for an allegiance of heart, mind and will. He constantly sets before his readers the element of choice, as here in John.1:12. Human beings are not by nature the spiritual children of God. I cannot 'become' something I am already. It is only by receiving Christ that I gain the right to become a child of God.

To Promise Life

The word 'life' in John is one of the most important to understand. The life the believer receives is not just the life we now live, going on for ever. It is the life of the eternal. 'In him was life' (John.1:4), and he came that we might have this life in abundance (John.10:10). The benefits of believing in him are that I may receive into my being the very life of God.

We need to understand that, in approaching this Gospel, as with any book in the Bible, we cannot do so in the manner we might approach an ordinary book, however great a genius the author may be. We have in our hands a book which sets out to persuade. And because it is a work into which God has breathed his Spirit, its deeper mysteries can only be fully received when we readily open our minds to its divinely inspired truth and the Spirit himself is pleased to reveal it.

Questions for Group Discussion:

1) In the light of 1Corinthians 2:6-16, consider the final paragraph of the above chapter.

2) How important do you rate external evidence when seeking to determine the authorship of the Gospel?

3) The next chapter introduces us to the text of the Gospel. How important do you think it is to establish the authorship,date and purpose of any book in the Bible before studying it?

CHAPTER 1

THE MAN WHO WAS SENT FROM GOD
c.John.1:6-8, 19-34; 3:22-36; 5:31-6.

In this study we are concerned with John the Baptist. So as not to confuse him with the author of the Gospel we will refer to him throughout as the Baptist.

When we consider the prologue to the Gospel (John1:1-14) in our next study, we shall see that John loses no time in introducing Jesus, the main subject of his Gospel. There are, however, three verses in the prologue which refer not to Jesus but to the Baptist, and there is a good reason for this. John is anxious to show that Jesus is the promised Messiah, the one who would redeem his people Israel and to whose coming the Old Testament prophets looked forward. The Baptist was the last of the Old Testament prophets and by bringing him into his Gospel at the very beginning John identifies his message closely with Jewish tradition. In any case, historically, it was the Baptist who introduced Jesus to the world he came to save.

Chapter 1:6 tells us who he was and that he was sent from God. In this way John stresses the authority which lay behind the Baptist's mission. Verse 7 tells us why he came. It was to testify to the light that was coming into the world so that everyone might believe (see also v.9). In verse 8, in order to avoid misunderstanding, John affirms that the Baptist was not the light but simply there to point men to it. This he does constantly, (v.15, 26, 30, 35). Because the Baptist represents the Old Testament, he must, now fade into the wings as Jesus takes centre-stage. The old covenant of the law is about to give way to the new covenant of grace. This is the significance of the Baptist's words in chapter 3:30. It is well worth our while to devote a chapter considering this incredible man who bridged the gap between the Testaments.

17

God *Prepared* His Messenger

Because John's Gospel supplements the synoptics, we must expect to find certain information in Matthew Mark and Luke that is not in John. In fact, St John's Gospel contains very little synoptic material. For example, Luke tells us two very interesting things about the Baptist.

a) He was subject to a special anointing of the Holy Spirit. The angel told Zechariah that his son would be 'filled with the Holy Spirit even from birth' (Luke 1:15b). This was, of course, very different from the birth of Christ, who was 'conceived by the Holy Spirit' (Luke 1:35). We need to remember that we are still in the Old Testament dispensation, when the Holy Spirit seems to have been given for some special work: For example, when Israel needed to be delivered from the King of Mesopotamia, we read that 'the Spirit of the Lord descended upon Othniel' (Judges 3:10). Similarly, when they needed deliverance from the Midianites, 'The Spirit of the Lord took possession of Gideon' (Judges 6:34), and 'the Spirit of the Lord came upon Jephtha in order to deliver them from the Amonites' (Judges11:29). This is why David felt able to pray 'take not your Holy Spirit from me' (Psalm 51:11). The Spirit came with the mission and departed when the mission was complete. With the Baptist,the Spirit began his work even before he was born. God was actually shaping his life in a very special way for a very special work.

b) The second interesting feature which Luke mentions is that,from his birth the Baptist was surrounded by the love and influence of the Spirit through his parents. In this he was tremendously privileged. Luke records how both Zechariah and Elizabeth were 'filled with the Holy Spirit' (Luke 1:41,67). It is a salutary reminder to all Christian parents that they too have a responsibility to keep faith with their God. It is an imponderable question, but how many potential servants of God have been lost to the church because of faithless parents? Sometimes one comes across 'roots out of dry ground'- lively Christian people who have gained little from the barren soil into which their lives were born. But they are not the norm.   They are tributes to the amazing grace of God.

The Messenger's Life was *Divinely Programmed*

This is another way of saying that God set a course for the Baptist's life to run, and he ran it.   He was indeed a man of destiny.

First, it was foretold in the Old Testament. 'I will send my messenger, who will prepare the way before me' (Malachi 3:1). 'I will send you the prophet Elijah before that great and dreadful day of the Lord comes, (Malachi 4:5; see also Isaiah40:30).

Secondly, it was fulfilled in the New Testament. Whatever interpretation we may like to put on these Old Testament passages, one thing is certain. Jesus saw them as a prophecy concerning the Baptist (see Matthew 11:10, 'This is the one about whom it was written'; or again in verse 14, 'If you are willing to accept it, he is the Elijah who was to come'). This, of course, does not mean that the Baptist was a reincarnation of Elijah.   The words have to be understood in the sense of Luke.1:76, where we read that he would go before the Lord in the spirit and power of Elijah. If Elijah was the rugged prophet of the Old Testament, the Baptist was undoubtedly his counterpart in the New. This all helps us to see how the arrival of the Baptist was part of the unfolding purposes of God. It is rather like a game of chess.   The master mind programmes the part each piece will play. Some are destined to be immobile guardians of an existing situation; some are very active darting here and there; some are sacrificed in the interest of winning through;while others will see the end of the contest. Some pieces have a variety of moves, just as some of God's children have many gifts. Others move with greater simplicity. Some will seem to have a considerable influence upon the progress of events, while others will be much less in evidence. Some will be active early in the game, while others await their call into play. So it was with the Baptist. He had a very special place in the economy of God. His appearance on the scene was at a significant time.His great work was to see out the Old Testament and usher in the New with the great cry, 'Look, the Lamb of God, who takes away the sin of the world' (Jn.1:29).

What is true for John the Baptist in a very real sense is true for all God's children. We are where we are because of what we are - God's children - and he has put is hand upon each one of us, to take our place in the great conflict against evil. There is a delightful verse in Luke 1:80 which says of the Baptist, 'He lived in the desert until he appeared publicly to Israel.' Perhaps God is saying to some of us, 'Your days in the desert are over; it is time you took an active role and bore your witness of me to the world.' The Baptist was very clear in his own mind as to his own commission from God (John.1:33-)4. There is, however, one further thing we should notice.

The Messenger was *Empowered* by God

The testimony of John the apostle was that the Baptist was sent from God (John 1:6) - literally, 'from alongside God'. The implication is that he enjoyed a close walk with God and was completely open to the prompting of the Holy Spirit. Furthermore, his life and witness gave evidence that he lived by the power of the Spirit. The strength of his virtuous life was well attested by Jesus, who said that he 'was a lamp that burned and gave light' (5:35). We live in a power hungry world and the thirst for power is insatiable. We are always talking about the balance of power, financial and autocratic power. Sadly we find it in the church: power to work miracles, to move congregations,to influence decisions, even to manipulate God. The Baptist was a man of power but not after this fashion. His power was that of a just and holy life. This is well brought out in Mark 6:18-20 when, after he had spoken boldly to Herod, 'it is not lawful for you to have your brother's wife', we read that 'Herod feared John ... knowing him to be a righteous and holy man'. His power was to make the sinner feel his guilt.

Questions for group discussion

1) To what extent would you say our lives are prepared and programmed by God for his work?

2) How does the Baptist support John's endeavour to show Jesus is Saviour, Messiah and God (consider 1:29-34; 3:27-36)?

3) The Baptist was above many things a very practical man as far as his faith was concerned. How would you illustrate this from Matthew 7:12 and Mark 6:14-25?

CHAPTER 2

PROLOGUE: THE REVELATION OF THE WORD
John1:1-14

John the Baptist was the one person who saw Jesus for who he really was and even he was confused at first (John 1:31), until it was revealed to him (v.33). From that moment he was confidently able to say, 'this is the Son of God' (v.34). It was not until the events at Caesarea Philippi (Matthew 16:13-17) that the mystery was revealed to the disciples. We should be careful to notice that in neither instance did those concerned reason it out for themselves - it had to be revealed to them (compare Matthew 16:17 with John 1:33). We can only know the things of God as he is willing to reveal them. This was certainly true in Paul's case (Galations 1:15-16), and he reminds us in 1Corinthians 2:14 that 'The man without the Spirit does not accept the things that come from the Spirit of God'. Perhaps this helps us to understand why it was that, everywhere Jesus went, eyebrows were raised and questions asked as to who he was.

'What have you to say about him?' questioned the pharisees of the blind man whom Jesus healed (John 9:17). 'Who is this? Even the waves and the sea obey him!', said the disciples (Mark4:41). 'Who is this that has wisdom and does mighty works?'said the astonished multitude (Mark.6:3). 'Who is this that forgiveness sins?' said the scribes as Jesus counselled the paralytic (Mark2:6-7). 'Who do you make yourself out to be?' said the pharisees to Jesus in the Temple. The truth about Jesus was first revealed to John the Baptist and then to the disciples, but to the people at large it remained a mystery. It is into this world that John comes with his Gospel. 'Light shines in the darkness, but the darkness has not understood it' (1:5).

John does not refer to the virgin birth of Christ. He has no need to as the matter rests on the synoptic testimony. What he does is to go straight into a declaration as to the deity of Christ. This is no less a stumbling-block today than it was in the days when John wrote his Gospel. Most heresies concerning the nature of Christ arise from man's inability to hold together two arms of the paradox, the real humanity and the revealed deity of Christ. How can Jesus be God and man at the same time? Some say that this is impossible, and in order to appear credible suggest all kinds of solutions. For example, Jehovah's Witnesses and Christadelphians would claim Jesus is neither one thing nor the other. He is clearly more than man but necessarily less than God. The humanist can accept that he was the greatest teacher and prophet but nevertheless a man. Others attribute deity to Christ but say that this is incompatible with manhood, and so Jesus becomes a sort of phantom. The great weakness of all these attempts to explain Christ is that they insist upon God being brought within the compass of a human mind. This one cannot do. How small does God have to be to become acceptable? It is not intellectual suicide to accept that God is beyond our capacity to comprehend. We can know a great deal about God, but at the end of the day there has to be much more than we can ever hope to understand. We cannot explain the fusion of deity and humanity, both of which are emphatic in the Prologue, but we can have the faith -ability to receive it as a revelation from God.

Before looking at the Prologue in detail we must turn our attention to the phrase 'the Word' (v.1). 'In the beginning',we are told, 'was the Word'. It is the Greek word logos. What does it mean, and why does John use it? Two things are very clear. First, the Word refers to Christ and, secondly, it meant something to the readers for whom the Fourth Gospel was written.

John's is a philosophical Gospel. It was written, as has already been mentioned, to refute a Gnostic-type heresy abroad at the time. The phrase 'the Word' was a term commonly used by intellectuals, especially in the first century, and is said to be found more than a thousand times in the writings of Philo. Although its precise meaning is somewhat obscure, it seems to have meant something like this: The word of wisdom, of knowledge, of understanding, i.e. the word of the philosopher, is the greatest virtue. To be able to think and say is better than to perform great deeds. Seeking the ear of the philosophers, John takes the current thought and attributes to Christ what they saw as the greatest virtue. Jesus is the visible expression of God's thoughts toward mankind. This is one reason why, in the great Christian liturgies, Hebrews 1:1-9 is read alongside the Prologue on Christmas Day. In the Bible we have the Word written, an expression of God's thoughts. In Jesus we have the Living Word made flesh and dwelling among us.

There are three aspects of Christ's deity mentioned in the Prologue. We shall consider them under three simple headings.

His *Essential* Deity *(vv.1-3, 14b).*

By this we mean that Jesus is God. 'The Word was with God and the Word was God' v.1. This is the most emphatic of all statements. It is sometimes pointed out by Jehovah's Witnesses that there is no article attached to the word 'God' in the original, and therefore they claim that it should read 'the Word was a God'. In this way, they insist, John does not claim deity for Christ. That, of course, is not so. To begin with, there is no indefinite article in the Greek language. Furthermore,the literal translation of the phrase would be 'and God was the Word', but because the subject has the article and the predicate does not, it is generally translated 'and God was the Word', In either case the deity of Christ is emphatic. Apart from this, the whole of the Gospel, as we shall see, is given over to establishing the deity of Christ.

John further emphasizes our Lord's deity by attributing to him the work of creation which, in the Bible, is only ascribed to the three persons of the Trinity, Father, Son and Holy Spirit. (compare John 1:3 with Job 33:4 and Acts 14:15). Creation is the prerogative of God. When John says 'We have seen his glory,the glory as of the one and only Son' (v.14) he is referring not only to our Lord's character but to his 'other worldliness'.It was the majesty, splendour and totality of heavenly radiance enshrining the Son which captivated their attention.

His *Eternal* Deity *(v.1a)*

'In the beginning was the Word (v.1.). At the very beginning of all things, Jesus was there. Before creation there was no time. Time began with creation. St Basil is renowned for his words, 'These two terms "beginning" and "was" are like two anchors at which the ship of a man's soul may safely ride whatever storms may come.' Then comes his most famous quote, 'There never was a time when Christ was not.' The birth of Jesus at Bethlehem was not his beginning: it was the way he came into this world. It was his arrival.

His *Ethical* Deity *(vv.4-5, 10).*

From the very beginning God has shown himself to be a moral being. By this we mean that there is right and wrong with God. There is a code of behaviour which is acceptable to God. This is known as righteousness or right behaviour. To behave otherwise is to be unrighteous. To misbehave knowingly is to be disobedient to God's law of righteousness and this incurs God's wrath. In the Old Testament the law of God was revealed through the prophets and written down. It was not until Jesus came that the righteousness of God was fully revealed in human nature, for he alone is without sin (Hebrews 4:15). Jesus, therefore, becomes to us the revelation of righteousness. It is not just his moral life that is wholly acceptable to the Father. His words are true, his decisions are right, and his judgements are perfect. This amazing revelation is the Light that has come into the world, and this Light is the very Life of God among men. He is in every way the 'express image of his (God's) person' (Hebrews 1:3). Just as a word is a sound image, a verbal picture of a thought, so 'the Word made flesh' is a visible image of the moral excellence of God. This is why Jesus alone can say' Anyone who has seen me has seen the Father' (John 14:9).

We cannot conclude this chapter without emphasising three things:

The *Mystery* of it.

Nicodemus is not the only person to ask the question 'How can this be?' It is too easy to dismiss what cannot be explained. The earnest seeker after truth will grasp what he can today and leave what he cannot for tomorrow. A child cannot understand the intricacies of a motor car. Indeed he may never understand, but he will accept it as a vehicle to ride in and enjoy, and perhaps later drive himself. The purpose of the car has been fulfilled and not lost on the child. However great our insights and understanding, we will always see through a glass darkly (1Corinthians 13:12). Who, in this nuclear age, will say that the mystery of life will for ever remain a mystery? What God does today he may, in his wisdom, enable man to understand tomorrow. It could be that, in his hunger for knowledge about the mysteries of God, mankind will never rise above seeing men 'as trees walking'. But the revealed truth remains, 'the Word became flesh' - a mystery indeed!

The *Simplicity* of it.

'And made his dwelling among us'. The living proof of this massive piece of theology, the fusion of the two natures, is seen in the simple fact that the baby Jesus was born and 'grew in wisdom and stature and in favour with God and men' (Luke 2:52), and confounded men with the unparalleled quality of his life. The natural birth of an unrecognized baby in an out-of-the-way corner in the

Middle East two thousand years ago could hardly have amounted, in those days, to a dramatic intrusion upon the world stage. His coming could not have been less obtrusive. How much more simple could it be? It was not until later, when he began to declare himself, that complications set in and individuals had to make decisions about him. Herod despised him, but the shepherds worshipped him. The Pharisees hated him, but Simeon and Anna offered their praises. Bethlehem shut her doors, but heaven sang. Pilate feared him, but Mary Magdalene loved him. The world crucified him, but the disciples believed him. What John does in this Gospel is to offer Christ in such away that his readers are compelled to make a decision about him.

The *Necessity* of it.
The personal appeal in this section comes in verses 11 to 13. The necessity of Christ's coming is that we who are estranged from God might become the children of God. Notice two things.
We may become 'children of God' (v.12). The word 'right' (NIV) is sometimes translated 'power' or 'authority'. It simply means that those who comply have a right to call themselves children of God because God says so.

We cannot become something we already are. If I am an artist, I obviously cannot become one. On the other hand, if I am not an artist, and this is my ambition, then I have to take the necessary steps to become one. John is not talking about becoming an artist, but a child of God in a special sense. Barrett, in his exhaustive Greek commentary, reminds us that 'Men are not by nature children of God, as for example by virtue of an indwelling. Only by receiving Christ do they gain the right to become children of God' (p.136). The phrase 'born of God' occurs frequently in the early chapters of John. It literally means being born from 'above', receiving new life that comes from God. Barrett also points that out 'It is of course a fundamental principle of gnostic thought that only the bestowal of light (knowledge) can give life (salvation)' (p.132).

This is another instance of John making use of current philosophical ideas to bring home the truth of the Gospel. It is not the word of knowledge but the Living Word who brings salvation.

How may we receive the life from above and thus become children of God? John fastens upon what appears to have been wrong thinking about these things. He points out in verse 13 that we do not become children of God by natural descent, that is by being the children of believers. Nor of human decision, that is simply by deciding to become a child of God. There is much more to regeneration than any decision I may wish to make about it. I can no more decide to become a child of God than I can decide to become a member of the royal family. Furthermore, no human agency can take on the responsibility for such a birth. I must be 'born of God'. After preaching on this theme on one occasion, a parishioner came up to me and said, 'You have completely destroyed my faith'. I was naturally saddened but asked the question, 'Is that a complaint or a discovery?' I am glad to report that it turned out to be a discovery, which is precisely what John is after in his Gospel: that men should discover their need of Christ, the only way of salvation.

The two words 'believed ' and 'received' (v.12), as the way to become the children of God, are fundamental in John. They mean accepting Christ in obedience and faith as the one sent from the Father. To those who do, the promise of life from above is given, and to them is given the right to say 'I am a child of God'.

Questions for Group Discussion

1) Who do you say Christ is? How would you describe him to someone who is totally ignorant of the Bible?

2) Discuss the statement 'to believe is to commit intellectual suicide'.

3) Share with one another what you understand by 'believing' and 'receiving'.

Chapter 3

SIGNS OF HIS DEITY

In chapters three to nine we are concerned with the miracle stories in the Gospel. We must, however, first give attention to the very special attitude John had toward the miracles of Jesus.

John's terminology

Whereas the synoptics generally use the word dynamis, mighty work, John invariably uses the word semeion, sign. To John our Lord's miracles were significant. But of what? They were signs of his deity and Messiahship. This is one reason why he was careful to mention that John the Baptist did no sign (10:41), emphasizing that he was not the expected Messiah. John also records how the Jews of his day associated miracles with Messiah who was to come. Twice they asked what sign he would give to prove his true identity (2:18, 6:30). Clearly, John saw our Lord's miracles, and intended his readers to see them, as evidence of his divine nature. With Jesus, what the prophet Isaiah foretold had come to pass (see Isaiah 29:18f). The Messianic age had dawned. Messiah had come and the miracles Jesus performed were evidence of it. It is perhaps surprising that Matthew ll:4-5 is not included among John's sayings of Jesus, since they fit perfectly into the prime appeal of the Gospel that Jesus is to be recognized as Messiah and Son of God through the miracles which he did.

The number seven

Because some commentators have drawn attention to the recurrence of the number seven in the Gospel, it seems appropriate to refer to the matter in passing. John records Jesus using the phrase 'I am' in a very special way, no less than seven times in connection with his divine attributes: e.g., 'I am the bread of life'. We shall consider this more closely when we study the discourses. There are, it is also pointed out, seven major discourses and seven miracles designated 'signs' in the first twenty chapters. The miracle of the draught of fishes in chapter 21 is not so designated. This strengthens the view that this particular chapter is an appendix to the Gospel but no less the work of John and equally inspired. Another point to notice is that it was not a miracle of his earthly ministry but of his resurrection. The importance of the number seven, biblical numerologists tell us, is that it is the perfect number, and as God alone is perfect we have in the sevenfold usage a clear indication of our Lord's deity. I am, however, of the opinion that not too much stress should be laid upon this kind of deduction as a way of establishing a theological truth. There are too many probabilities, and it is questionable as to whether the Bible should be subjected to this kind of treatment, especially when it is not specifically stated as, for example, in John's other work, Revelation 13:18. It is far better to rest our theological conclusions on the clear and precise statements in Scripture, and throughout these studies this is what we shall seek to do.

To elicit faith

The miracles in John's Gospel are not only foremost in setting forth the deity and Messiahship of Christ; they also illustrate how an unfolding of the truth about Jesus draws forth faith, and as a result new life is given. A notable distinction between the synoptic Gospels and John is that whereas in the first three Gospels, particularly in the healing miracles, the emphasis rests largely upon the benefits to those healed, in John the stress is very much upon the one who does the healing. The reader's mind is intentionally focused upon Christ. It will be seen how the declaration of John 20:31 is in every way fulfilled. This verse must always be kept in mind as we consider each sign in turn.

The all-sufficiency of Christ

Not once in the Gospel does Jesus call on the Father for his enabling. Jesus is seen to work in his own right and by his own divine power. He needed to give credit to no one, not even the Father. In the case of Lazarus (ll:25f), his prayer to the Father was relative to the belief of the bystanders, not a cry for help in performing the miracle. The disciples may have need of help as in Acts 3:6, 'In the name of Jesus Christ of Nazareth, walk', but not so Jesus. In this way John stresses the uniqueness of Jesus as the source of all life and power.

FIRST SIGN: WATER INTO WINE *(2:1-11)*

We must resist the temptation to embark upon a verse by verse analysis. There are, however, certain phrases in the account which must be commented upon. The first is in verses 2 and 3. Jesus, his mother and the disciples were invited as guests to a normal, happy, social occasion. It reminds us that Jesus was totally identified as a human being within human society. He was not, as some have suggested, deity striding the earth but apart from it. He was actually born into the human race and was truly man. St Paul speaks of Jesus as 'being found in human form' (Philippians 2:8). John's presentation of Jesus, paradoxically enough, is of a very human Jesus. In chapter 8:40 Jesus actually speaks of himself as a man: 'Now you are seeking to kill me, a man who has spoken the truth to you'. This is certainly how his enemies saw him, as John readily reminds us in chapter 10:33, 'You being a man make yourself God'. Leon Morris points out (New Testament Theology p 245) that his 'whole way of life is human' in the Gospel of John (consider 4:6; 19:26-7;7:3-5; 12:27; 11:5,35) Jesus was completely involved in the world and with the people he came to save. By inference he must therefore be equally concerned about me and the details of my life. He knows the path

I tread, the things I fear, the hopes I cherish and he holds in his hand the answer to all my needs.

However, it is not his humanity but his deity with which the evangelist is primarily concerned (v11). The sign manifested the glory which he shared with the Father before the incarnation (17:5,24). The significant aspect of the miracle was his control over creation. In the bible, as we saw in the previous chapter, the work of creation is attributed only to the Father, the Son and the Holy Spirit and to none other (Acts14:15; John 1:3; Job 33:4). The importance of the miracle was not simply to avert a crisis but to reveal a Christ. The need for more wine was not the cause of a miracle but the occasion of a 'sign'. Only God can manipulate His creation. Here, then,is God at work.

What was the reaction of the people? Of the general company who gathered, we are told nothing. We may assume without fear of challenge that there was much relief and surprise on the part of those who were 'in the know'. They were involved in a miracle but for the most part had no idea that it had taken place, or that a 'sign' had been given whereby they might have come to know their God. We are told, however, that the disciples who were in close touch with everything Jesus did, 'put their faith in him'. They recognized him for who he was, the Messiah who would come. It was as though, as in the transfiguration, the veil of his humanity had been momentarily moved aside, scales were lifted from their eyes and they were enabled to see the divine majesty that was vested in Christ. And they believed. In the midst of a world that is totally blind to the truth about Jesus, we need so much to pray that God will help us to see the truth that alone can set us free.

Questions for group discussion

1) 'Jesus did many other miraculous signs...but these are written...' (20:30-1). On what basis do you think John made his selection?

2) Why do you think Mary had such confidence that Jesus would be able to deal with the crisis? You may find it helpful to refer to Luke 1:35; 2:19,40,51.

3) How would you say that this miracle encourages us in our daily prayers?

4) To what do you think Jesus was referring when he said 'My time has not yet come'? There are other references to his time having come (see, for example, 7:30; 8:20; 12:23,27; 13:1; 17:1).

5) How is God at work in the world today? Does he still reveal his glory through his works in the same way? If he does, why do you think so few people seem to believe?

Chapter 4.

SECOND SIGN: HEALING THE NOBLEMAN'S SON *(4:43-54)*

Following the incident of turning the water into wine, our Lord visited Jerusalem, where many believed because of the signs he accomplished there (2:23). He came again to Galilee where, at Cana, he had already demonstrated the creative power of the Gospel. A nobleman begged him to go to Capernaum to heal his son who was apparently near to death. Jesus, however, did not go. Instead, He declared to the official, 'Go, your son will live'. The nobleman took the words of Jesus on trust and on returning home he found his son well and fully recovered. The consequence was that he and his whole household believed and became Christians.

In this second sign the emphasis is very different from that of the first. We have witnessed our Lord's power over nature; now we are to see his power over life. It is interesting to notice how often, after John records the first sign, he sets Jesus forth as the giver of life. He promises to raise up his body, the living Temple (2:13-22); he offers new birth and eternal life to Nicodemus (3:1-21); he again offers eternal life to those who believe (v36); he speaks of eternal life to the woman at the well of Sychar (4:14) and here in the second sign he restores to the nobleman's son a new quality of life. Whether it is physical, spiritual, temporal or eternal life, Jesus is its source and sustainer. As the Book of Common Prayer recognizes, God alone is the 'giver of all life'. Once again John offers Jesus to his readers as God, and the miracle is proof of it.

The one thing we are not going to do at this stage is anticipate the discourse on eternal life. What we can do is observe two very important elements in the miracle. The first is the link between believing and healing, and the second is to note how Jesus drew out the nobleman's faith.

Believing and healing

What is the link between believing and healing? The Bible is full of paradoxes. By just taking a verse or two it can be shown that miracles are impossible without some kind of faith. For example, we read in Matthew 13:58 'He did not do many mighty works there because of their unbelief'. Jesus himself said to Martha at a time when she seemed to be entirely without faith, 'Did I not tell you that if you believed you would see the glory of God?' (John 11:40). The implication is that without belief the glory of God would not be revealed. Belief comes first. But apparently this is not always so. There is no mention of faith or believing on the part of the impotent man before he was enabled to take up his pallet and walk in Chapter 5. There is no single or corporate act of faith which pre-empted the feeding of the five thousand in Chapter 6. Likewise, in Chapter 9 there is no demand for a statement of belief from the blind man before his sight was restored. Perhaps the one thing we can learn from this is that God will not be tied down. He is not predictable, and if he chooses to demonstrate his power independently on some occasions, there are other times when he demands faith. Our problems begin when we try to use God as a word-processor. You tap certain keys and it has to react in a certain way because that is how the computer is programmed. God is not programmed. Too many of us try to manipulate God in this way and in doing so we reduce God to a robot. I remember once going into a meeting- it was highly charged emotionally - and there was a man on his knees in the middle of the aisle banging his fist on the floor and crying out, 'God, you've got to do it, you've got to do it'. I don't know what it was that God had to do, and I don't know what would have happened if he hadn't done it, but I do know that God doesn't have to do anything that he chooses not to do. When it comes to faith and healing, the Bible shows us that there are times when God requires faith and times when he seems to extend his mercy without it. How wonderful is the grace of God! Nevertheless, in the miracle before us there is a close link between faith and healing. Whoever this man was, and there is no certainty he was the centurion of Luke 7 and Matthew 8, he comes to Jesus very deficient in matters of faith. Unlike the centurion, he assumes that in order for the healing to take place, it would be necessary for Jesus to travel to Capernaum. He certainly does not believe that Jesus could help his son if he died, and so he urges him to hurry before it is too late. But Jesus reveals yet a further deficiency in his faith and challenges him 'Unless you see signs and wonders you will not believe'. In the Greek the word means 'definitely not' believe. Then what kind of a faith did this man have? The one thing we do know is that somehow he had heard that Jesus could work miracles of healing and so he comes to the healer on behalf of his son. In every way understandable and commendable but in no way approaching what Jesus had in mind in verse 48 when he spoke about believing. The man's faith was on the bottom rung of the ladder. Having been offered this mild rebuke we read that 'the man believed the word Jesus spoke to him and went his way' (v.50). C.K.Barrett (St John p205) puts it extremely well when he describes 'the man's faith in this way satisfied with this assurance, the officer returned home'.What then can we conclude from all this?

Surely the first thing is that Jesus felt able to respond to this man's need even though his faith was no more than believing his son would be healed as long as he followed the instructions given. This seems to be the meaning of the latter part of verse 50. There is another factor, however. Jesus,who knew all things from the beginning to the end, was fully aware that it was incipient faith, that is, it was the beginning of a deeper faith which would eventually embrace him as the Son of God, the author of all life. This surely is the 'belief' of verse 53. It has to be an immense encouragement to all of us who have sincere difficulties in the realm of faith, to know that God does not always wait for maturity in Christian experience before he lavishes his grace upon us. Quality of faith has to be of greater importance than quantity. The kind of faith God is looking for has to be sincere and capable of growth. It cannot be lost in any form of selfishness, and ultimately will find its full expression in a total surrender in love for God and his will.

The development of faith

This is not the only occasion when Jesus seems to rebuke or even turn his back on a genuine approach for help. The Syrophoenician woman in Mark 7:24-30 had the same experience. If you look carefully you will see that Jesus was pressing her into a self-examination of her faith. She persisted, and her sincerity was rewarded. When she returned home and found her child had been relieved of the demon possession, her own faith in, and love for, Christ must have become ten times stronger.But it had all been there in embryo in the first instance. We may say the same thing for the nobleman. I once studied this passage with a group of young teenagers and to make it simple I traced the incident through, asking them to note the following: Request, (verse 47b); Rebuke, (48); Reality, (49); Reply, (50a);Response, (50b); Reward, (51); and Renewal, (53). At the end of the study I asked them to write down in a short sentence what the incident taught about faith. One reply, and far and away the most interesting, was from a thirteen year-old who wrote: 'Not a lot about faith, but a lot about Jesus'. Exactly! It could hardly have been more profound. In the incident he saw Jesus at work, bringing this nobleman through from small and unenlightened faith to great trust and commitment. Remember, these things are written that we might believe that Jesus is the Christ. This is what the nobleman came to understand and accept. The question is, Have we yet come to that place where our faith has risen sufficiently to commit our lives to him as God and Saviour?

This is My Son

Questions for group discussion

1) Compare the passage above with Matthew 8:5-13 and Luke 7:1-10. Note the similarities and differences between the Johanine and synoptic accounts. Do you think they are different accounts of the same incident? If so, why? If not, why not?

2) How would you say that the divine nature of Jesus is revealed in this incident?

3) Discuss the phrase, 'the strength of faith depends on its object'.

THIRD SIGN: HEALING THE PARALYTIC *(5:1-18)*.

In the first two signs Jesus declared his divine nature by his control over creation and over life. This third sign brings in another important element, his authority over the law. It also shows how divisive his miracles were. Yet a third point of interest is that whereas in the first two signs he was approached, here it is Jesus who does the approaching. The pool of Bethesda is there for all to see in Jerusalem today, and thousands must have read this story as they sat within the precincts and experienced the excitement of imagining it all taking place before their very eyes. The passage is in three parts. Verses 2-9 record the miracle; 10-16 the Sabbath controversy; and 17-18 the declaration Jesus made concerning his equality with the Father.

His *Compassion (vv 2-9)*

We have already noticed that it is Jesus who approached the paralytic. Why did he do this? Whatever reasons we may offer, we have to accept that it is in the nature of God to love his creation and here we have an instance of that love. John records, 'God so loved the world' (3:16). This means that God loves me, and Christ's approach to the paralytic is indicative of it. If we follow the story right through we see many expressions of God's compassion. In verse 6 Jesus approaches him at a moment when he was least expecting anyone to come to his aid. The incarnation itself is the most amazing approach God ever made to his creation. This too was at a time when his coming was unexpected by nearly all of Israel. It is the sort of thing which God does. In verses 6-7 Jesus engaged him in conversation: 'The Word was made flesh and made his dwelling among us' (1:14). What he had to say, touched the deepest need of which the paralytic was aware. In verse 14, however, we see an even deeper need relating to the forgiveness and forsaking of sin. And who can forgive sins but God? This is yet another reflection upon the deity of Christ. In verse 8 he heals the man of his physical sickness, a forerunner of that greater healing he was soon to understand. In verses 13-14 Jesus follows him to encourage him in his new found freedom, and finally in verse 14 our Lord encourages him to go on in his spiritual awakening.

The words in verse 14, 'sin no more, that nothing worse befall you', need a little explanation. There is no suggestion that his sickness was a consequence of sin, and could well be understood in the light of chapters 9:3 and 11:4. The phrase 'sin no more', however, reminds us of another paralytic Jesus healed in Mark 2:9, where he says 'Your sins are forgiven'. There is no direct mention of forgiveness in the story, but the command to sin no more suggests that his sins had already been forgiven.

His *Authority* (vv.10-16)

Jesus is not actually breaking Jewish law concerning the Sabbath. He is encouraging someone else to break it. In other words he assumed an authority which is above Jewish law. There had been an extraordinary development of the Mishna (a compilation of precepts passed down as an oral tradition and later forming part of the Talmud) from the original law which was given to Moses Under Jewish law it was not permissible to remove an article from one house to another on the Sabbath. If, however, a sick person was on a pallet, removal would be allowed as the pallet is secondary to the person carried and it is perfectly in order fora person to move from one house to another. Jesus could have suggested to the paralytic that he went home and returned for his bed the next day, but it seems the he was seeking to make a point. To Jesus this was an absurd hedging of the law which put a burden upon the people - not intended as the law was originally given. The two things to note, then, are these:

First, Jesus assumed an authority above accepted Jewish tradition. Secondly, he adopted an attitude toward the Sabbath, better expounded in the synoptics than in John, that the Sabbath was made for man and not man for the Sabbath: that is, the law was given to encourage virtue, not to restrict it (see Luke13:10-17; 14:1-6; Mark 2:27-28). Without going into theological details, John is saying that a greater than the Temple itself was among them (see Matthew 12:5-8).

His *Deity (vv.17-18)*

Those who claim that there is no clear statement in the Bible as to the deity of Christ, and therefore deny the doctrine of the Father, Son and Holy Spirit in Trinity, would do well to study the Fourth Gospel in depth. Whatever conclusion we may draw from the words of Jesus, those who heard him were in no doubt whatever as to the claims which he made for himself. He made himself equal with God, and he did not deny this. In verses 19-24 we have a very clear statement as to what Jesus understood by equality with God, especially verses 21-23. It is important to notice how once again John brings together all the elements of chapter 20:31, culminating in the statement that forgiveness and eternal life come through belief in Christ (v.24).

Questions for discussion

1) In conversation with an unbeliever I was asked, 'If God loved the world, why did he go about selecting people for healing?' Can your study group agree on a brief paragraph in answer to this question?

2) How would you interpret 'The Sabbath was made for man' for today's society?

3) How many allusions do you see to the deity of Christ in verses 1-24?

Chapter 5

FOURTH SIGN: FEEDING THE FIVE THOUSAND *(6:1-14)*

The miracle of the feeding of the five thousand is the only miracle story recorded in all four Gospels. Because John's was the last to be written, and the evangelist had the synoptic accounts at hand, it would seem that he had a particular reason for giving it this special treatment. One cannot pontificate upon the reasons, but it can be pointed out that a significant feature is that John alone mentions it was at Passover time. This has to be theologically important and we shall consider the implications when we study the discourse on the Bread of Life. The account of the miracle in John is also followed by the first and most divisive (see vv.60-66) of his seven discourses, where the use of 'I am' is followed by a series of predicates, in this case 'the Bread of Life'. Of all the miracles, the feeding of the five thousand is the most difficult for the sceptic to accept and lends itself most readily to alternative interpretations. On the other hand, assuming one retains the miraculous element, it is the most convincing as far as establishing the true nature of Christ is concerned. We have therefore a very strong reason for its inclusion in the Fourth Gospel. Again John says to his readers, 'This is indeed the Christ', for, to him, the feeding of the five thousand is the miracle of miracles. It is truly a sign for all to see and understand. When the people saw the sign which Jesus had done, they said, 'This is indeed the prophet who is to come into the world' (v.14). They associated the miracle with the promise given through Moses in Deuteronomy 18:15f.

An inadequate view of the miracle.

The author finds it sad that so many otherwise splendid commentaries fail to offer to their readers any confidence in the event as a true miracle. What is more disturbing is that they do not always offer an alternative explanation. The most common suggestion is that what really happened was that when Jesus took the loaves and fishes from the lad and blessed them and distributed them among those who had no food, it inspired everyone else who had food with them to share it with others. The miracle was the change of heart that came over the people, and the amount of food that was left over was a sharp lesson that in the world there was enough for all. The total inadequacy of his view is manifest when one looks closely into the record. First of all, it has to be said that all four Gospels make it very clear that a miracle actually took place. Certainly, as far as John was concerned, without a miracle you do not have a 'sign'. Secondly, it is doubtful whether simply bringing about a change of heart and giving a practical demonstration on 'there is more than enough for everyone' would have been anything like sufficient for the multitude to be persuaded that Jesus was the prophet who was to come (v.14), let alone stir up the people to make him King (v.15). To John, Jesus was doing much more than controlling the hearts of men; he was controlling his creation.

Difficulty in accepting miracles

In Chapter 2 we maintained that it is not intellectual suicide to receive what comes as a revelation from God even though it is beyond our capacity to comprehend. We were thinking about the person of Christ and the conflict between his humanity and deity. This is no less true of miracles. For some years I worked with physicists, and was involved in research work in the field of electronics. All scientists accept the basic principle that nothing is impossible. Once you determine anything to be totally impossible, you close for ever the door of research and discovery. If you drop the word 'miracle' from your theological vocabulary, you shut your mind and soul to a huge area of divine possibilities. In effect you say 'God cannot'. This is the very point the angel was making to Mary in Luke 1:36-7, With God nothing is impossible'. Jesus went even further when he said, 'What is impossible with men is possible with God' (Luke 18:270. There is no valid, let alone intellectual, reason for not accepting the record of the feeding of the five thousand as a miracle, and as such, a sign of his deity and Messiahship.

The Kingdom

Apart from the confession of Nathaniel in chapter 1:49, in verse 15 we have the first mention of the kingship of Christ, and even here it is the perception of Christ and not a cry of the people. It is a title commonly used of Jesus in the passion narratives in the Gospel. Jesus's view of the King coming in his kingdom was at variance with the common Messianic conception. This expectancy was of an earthly kingdom that would be set up, headed by a prophet of great distinction who would free the Jewish people from the yoke of the Romans and establish the nation in its own right in justice and peace. Jesus, however, did not seek to emulate David of the Old Testament by re-establishing the Jewish kingdom as the Jews both wanted and expected of Messiah. He came to set up a kingdom in the hearts of men, and join them to himself in righteousness and faith. A study of the verbal conflict he had with Pilate in chapter 18:33-9 draws out clearly the distinction in ideas. This, of course, is why Jesus withdrew to the mountains (v.15). In the Gospel the materialistic attitude of the Jews in matters of faith and practice is consistently contrasted with the deeper and more spiritual emphasis of Jesus (see 2:20; 3:4; 6:15; 8:21-2).

A devotional challenge

Bible students should always be wary of spiritualizing, that is, by passing the clear and factual intention of the passage and looking for some excuse to bring out a devotional 'gem'. This is not only to misuse the Bible but also to open the gateway to some very strange theology. However, this does not mean that there are no devotional thoughts in the Scriptures. Indeed, the Bible is full of them, and I would commend such authors as William Temple, Matthew Henry and George Hutcheson as among the best in helping us in this area of study. One helpful way of understanding the way God deals with us, is to observe how he deals with people in the Bible. We have a very good example here. Focus your attention on the lad with the loaves and fishes. What he had, the Lord needed (v.9). Perhaps there is a possession or a talent we have, that at present has not been handed over to the Lord. What he offered, the Lord blessed (v.11). One never knows how the Lord will sanctify the service we render him, any more than the woman who put two mites into the treasury (Luke 21:2). What the Lord blesses, he multiplies (v.12), that is, he touched others in ever-widening ripples. In this case he dealt with their hunger. Who knows how far and wide God will take, bless and spread our offerings, however small and whatever they may be? To this day we are touched by the quality of giving displayed by that woman at the treasury. Her example still compels us to consider the elements of sacrifice and self-effacement in all our service for Christ.

Questions for discussion

1) Apart from mentioning that the miracle took place around Passover time, what other additions to the story are found in John when compared with the synoptics? (Note especially v.14;the other passages are Matthew 14:13-21; Mark 6:30-44; Luke 9:10-17). What importance do you attach to the additions?

2) How would you reply to someone who said, 'I just don't believe in miracles'?

3) Why do you think Jesus rejected the people's attempt to make him King?

FIFTH SIGN: WALKING ON THE WATER *(6:16-21)*.

So far, in dealing with the four previous signs, we have no doubts that we are concerned with 'miracles'. What is generally regarded as the fifth sign, however, may not necessarily have been a miracle at all. We don't even have the suggestion from John that he regarded it as a 'sign'. It certainly is not described as such in the Gospel, neither is there any suggestion that 'belief' resulted from it. This is all the more remarkable, as in every other instance someone 'believed' as a consequence of the miracle (see 2:11; 4:53; 5:14,24; 6:14; 9:38;11:40,42). If we hold to the full inspiration of the Bible, as the writer of this book does, there is no way in which we will question the possibility of miracles, but we must not fall into the trap of making a miracle out of an event for the sake of it. Does Jesus have to walk 'on' the water? Not necessarily so, according to John. The words which John uses in 6:19 are identical in the original language to those used in 21:1, and nobody would dream of translating 21:1 as 'on' the sea - but 'by' it. Bearing in mind the two important factors mentioned above,that the miracle is not designated a 'sign' and there is no record of 'belief' arising from it, what grounds have we for regarding the occasion as a miracle? The answer probably lies in the synoptic record of the same incident (Matthew 14:22-36;Mark 6:45-56), where Jesus is clearly said to have walked 'on' the water. It seems less likely that these hardened sailors would have been frightened if they had been close to land, in which case *epi* should be translated 'on' rather than 'by'. Hendriksen, Barrett and others are at pains to point out that having rowed some three to four miles, according to the Johanine record, the disciples would still have been the best part of a mile off shore when the event took place. Our submission is that this was yet a further miracle and sign of our Lord's authority over his creation. The reference to 'signs' and 'belief' are to be found in verses 29-30, which mark the beginning of his great discourse on the Bread of Life. John, once again, is happy to rest his case on the synoptic testimony and sees no need to stress the miraculous element in the story. In any case, his use of the word *epi* can justifiably be understood to mean 'on' without violating the mother tongue of the Gospel. There is no conflict with existing traditions.

Jesus had withdrawn himself to the mountains to pray (v.15;Mark 6:48). In spite of his preoccupation, the darkness, and the distance from his disciples, he was yet aware of their distress. It recalls the reaction of Hagar in Genesis 16:7-14,when she discovered the Lord as the one who sees. Surely this is a matter of discomfort to the sinner but of great consolation to the believer. Many would see in the disciples' gladness to take the Lord on board (v.21), a beautiful picture of receiving Christ into one's life in the fullest Johanine sense. This has to be admissible, but John would want us to realize that it was as Saviour, Messiah and Son of God that he comes (see again 20:31).

Questions for discussion

1) Discuss the statement, 'Contrary to John supplementing the synoptics, here we have the synoptics supplementing John.' What is the importance of this observation?

2) Why were the disciples frightened in verse 19? Can you imagine a situation in which you might justifiably be fearful of Jesus?

Chapter 6

SIXTH SIGN: HEALING THE MAN BORN BLIND *(9:1-12)*.

There are a number of basic observations which must be made before we examine this miracle of healing. First of all, we notice Jesus takes the initiative and approaches the man of his own volition. He does so in order that God may be seen to be at work in him (v.3). Faith is not asked for in the first instance but, as we have seen earlier, the man healed was capable of great faith (ch.4, 'Believing and Healing'). It is also a rare occasion where Jesus uses means to cure, in this case spittle mixed with dust from the ground (see also Mark.7:33; 8:23). There is no clue as to why Jesus adopted this method and there is certainly no consensus of opinion among biblical scholars. Some say that he used a cure not unknown to contemporary medicine,while others affirm that there was no more healing in the clay than there was in the waters of the Jordan, which were used to cure Naaman the leper (2 Kings 5). Perhaps one should remember,however, that the waters of the Jordan have a very high salt content and its healing qualities are not altogether unknown. Another suggestion offered is that Jesus was identifying himself with his original work of creation when Adam was made from the dust of the ground (Genesis 2:5-7). This is a point which John would not be slow to miss. We might also conclude that Jesus was giving the 'Amen' to the use of a well-tried medical practice. It would have certainly stirred an element of hope and expectancy in the sick man, and any psychologist would stress the importance of instilling confidence in healing sicknesses of a psychosomatic nature. It was not that Jesus needed an 'aid' to healing, but that any means used also requires his aid. Hence, 'In the name of Jesus Christ of Nazareth, walk' (Acts 3:6). The disciples could not go it alone.

Sin and sickness.

In verse 2, the question of the relationship between sin and sickness is once again raised. It is a fact that certain diseases resulting from sexual abuse and promiscuity can cause blindness, so the issue may not altogether be lost in local superstition. It could have been a recognized phenomenon of the time. But Jesus was careful to point out that it was not the case with this man. John, in his eagerness to set forth Jesus as the Christ, the Son of God, was quick to record the words of our Lord, 'not this man or his parents but that the works of God may be manifest in him' (v.3). If we allow that all sickness is a consequence of a fallen society, we must insist that it is not necessarily the result of a direct sin on the part of the sufferer. Suffering is sometimes the result of somebody else's sin (Exodus 20:5). The passage does not lead us into the question of suffering as a result of a disaster, such as an earthquake.

Spiritual blindness

The reader will have noticed that in considering the 'signs' we have deliberately avoided becoming involved in the discourses which often followed them. In verse 5, Jesus states that he has come as Light into a world of darkness. His teaching on 'Light' occurs throughout the Gospel and we shall give our attention to this in a later chapter, but we do well to notice at this juncture that the blind man's physical healing is not set forth as the major theme. True, his eyes were opened, thus enabling him to see the world around him; but an even greater vision came to him. He could now see something which the Jews in their spiritual blindness could not see. He could see the truth about Jesus, and he believed (v.38). There is no instance in the Gospel which expresses 20:31 better than the healing of the man born blind.

A time for decision

There are three conversations here. The first is between the Jews and the man healed. The second is between the Jews and the man's parents. The third between the man and Jesus. In the second conversation with the parents, the Jews simply wanted to confirm the accuracy of the reports that had reached them (vv.18-23). Not wishing to be put out of the synagogue themselves, they confirmed the facts but refused to be drawn on a theological issue. The discussion with the man, however, is very revealing. They could not dispute that he had been made to see but, wishing to discredit Jesus, they raised two objections. The first was the Sabbath issue. Jesus had actually made clay, and the kneading of dough on the Sabbath was strictly forbidden, (Shabbath 7:2). The second objection was that he taught contrary to Moses (v.29), and so they referred to him as a sinner(v.24). Their point was that it was impossible to be a disciple of Moses and Jesus at the same time. With this they put the man healed on the spot, and he openly had to make a firm decision for himself. This is true for all of us. Once faced with the claims of Christ, we have to make a decision about him. We either accept his divine Lordship or we reject it. To shelve the issue is to refuse to accept him and, as the writer to the Hebrews reminds us, 'How shall we escape if we ignore such a great salvation?' (Hebrews 2:3).

Personal faith

In the case of the man born blind, it all began with an unexpected meeting on the highway, when, out of the blue, Jesus healed him of his physical blindness. During the ensuing conversation with the Jews he confesses that he believes Jesus to be some kind of prophet (v.17). His was not a sudden conversion to full commitment. It was gradual, but it was enough for him to exercise boldness and severely challenge what to him was the blind, irrational stupidity of the Jews (vv.30-3). No wonder they cast him out. They actually helped him into the kind of faith John would call 'believing' and 'receiving'. When the Lord approached him later and openly told him who he was (v.37),he gladly surrendered his life fully and worshiped Jesus (v.38). In this story we have a remarkable contrast. The 'sign' which helped the man healed of physical blindness to see the truth about Jesus, had the reverse effect upon the Jews. They too witnessed the 'sign' of Christ's divine nature but rejected the revelation. They made their decision and the 'sign' condemned them as blind. Marsh has a telling phrase (commentary on St. John p390), 'Seeing, in the sense of believing, or being blind in the sense of not believing is a fully voluntary and responsible act of the human person'. That being so, and we believe it is,we can only end this study with the words of Jesus to the man who gained his sight, 'Do you believe in the Son of Man?' (v.35).

Questions for discussion

1) How do you see the relationship between prayer and the application of medical science?

2) Discuss the phrase, 'From earliest times suffering is often seen as the result of somebody else's sin, and it isn't fair.'

3) How does this chapter bring out the need for personal faith in conversion?

SEVENTH SIGN: THE RAISING OF LAZARUS *(11:1-44)*.

There are three occasions recorded in the Gospels when Jesus raised someone from death to life: the daughter of Jairus (Mark5:21-43; Matthew 9:18-26; Luke 8:40-56), the widow's son at Nain (Luke 7:11-17) and Lazarus in (John 11:17-27). There is no reason for identifying the Lazarus of John with Luke.16:19-31 -the setting for this miracle is in verses 1-4. On being told of Lazarus' sickness, Jesus again establishes that the occasion is for the glory of God and that the Son of God (Himself) may be glorified through it'. The delay of two days (v.6) can be accounted for by the need for Lazarus to have died (vv.14-15). To raise Lazarus from the dead was no more difficult for Jesus than it would be for anyone else to awaken someone from natural sleep. Instead of using the words 'to awake him out of sleep',he could just as well have said 'to bring him back to life' (vv.11b-13). The meaning of the narrative for John is primarily that Jesus has authority to give life. This is something only God can do. He is, however, not only the life-giver, but also the life given (v.25). We will look into this theme a little more closely when we think together about our Lord's teaching on eternal life.

The road to Jerusalem

There is a sense in which the miracle is climactic because it was the cause which finally led to the crucifixion (vv.45-53). In John, as indeed in all three synoptics, Calvary is no accident, and the determination of Jesus to walk that road as part of the plan of salvation is evident in this chapter as elsewhere in the Gospel. In verses 7-8 and 15-16, even in the face of Jewish threats, the disciples were unable to dissuade him. It is very interesting to compare references 7:5-8, 11:54-6 and 12:9-14. The most direct statement on our Lord's intent to walk the Calvary road is to be found in Luke 9:51-3. The disciples, not yet understanding that Jesus must suffer (24:25-7) can be forgiven if at first they assumed that his fixed purpose was just to awaken Lazarus out of sleep. The Good Shepherd, however,came to lay down his life for the sheep. The crucifixion was never far from the Lord's mind, and for him the hour had come. The raising of Lazarus was essentially a miracle which Jesus performed on the way to Calvary.

Seeing the Glory of God

Brief reference was made to this when we considered the prologue in chapter 2. One of the great claims John made was that he had actually seen the glory of God in Christ (John 1:14;

see also 1John 1:1-2). Of what did the promise which Christ made to Mary in verse 40 consist? It was certainly not the miracle itself because the opportunity had not arisen. At no time is Christ's working of miracles described as God's glory. Rather, the miracles point to the glory and there does not have to be a miracle for anyone to see that glory. Miracles are no more than a 'sign' of it. The glory of God in Christ will never be better expressed than in the most stirring of all carols, 'Hark the herald angels sing, glory to the new-born King', where we have the line 'Veiled in flesh the Godhead see'. And when, through faith, a person can say of Christ 'I see in him the fullness of God', as for example in Colossians 1:15-19, and commits himself or herself to it, then that person is a true believer in the sense of verse 40. John is concerned that his readers should set their sights beyond the miracles to what they signify, the true majesty of the Eternal God in Christ. Jesus was equally concerned about this, as we see in chapter 6:26-7.

Christ, the divider of men

We saw in the previous miracle how people's reactions to Jesus differed. This is never more apparent than in the incident before us. It was the last straw which drove the Sanhedrin, under the influence of Caiaphas, to decide firmly that Chris must go. There is a telling phrase in verses 45 and 46, 'Many of the Jews therefore believed in him, but some went to the Pharisees'. Reactions were very different as they have always been. The belief of some does not necessarily indicate that they had a deep understanding or that there was full commitment(see 2:22-5), but there was certainly enough for the chief priests and Pharisees to sense a loyalty to Jesus as the possible Messiah which both threatened their position and the future of the nation. They would argue, 'How could a sinner who disagreed with Moses possibly be the Messiah?' However, we do the Pharisees, who were purists at heart, an injustice if we judge them to be totally bad.

Their main problem was not that they were evil, but blind. Fanaticism was, and still is, the hallmark of many religions. Disagreement was met with hostility, often of a very sinister kind. Jesus was to warn his disciples of this in the Upper Room when he said to them 'The hour is coming when whoever kills you will think he is offering service to God (16:2), and for Jesus the hour had come. The irony of the whole drama was that the very thing which they hoped to avoid, came to pass - the dispersion of the Jewish nation and destruction of the Temple.   What they hoped to destroy - the influence of Jesus and his followers - took root and flourished.

God's plan and theirs

A remarkable feature of this story is that the words of Caiaphas in verse 50 'It is expedient for you that one man should die for the people', could equally well have been spoken by God. The death of Christ was essential to the purposes of God, as well as to the subtle plan of Caiaphas. The aim, however, was vastly different. It is important that we can discern the difference and give an answer for the faith we have, but this we will leave for the questions below.

Questions for discussion

1) How do you assess the faith of Martha and Mary (vv. 21,32-40,45)?

2) How would you explain the meaning of verse 40 to an unbeliever?

3) 'Caiaphas was made an unconscious vehicle of truth' (Barrett p.339).   Discuss this.

Chapter 7

THE TEACHING OF JESUS

In John's Gospel, miracles are 'signs' of our Lord's deity and Messiahship, pointers as to who he really was, the Son of God,the one who should come to redeem Israel.We should now be asking the question, How do I view Christ,and has the Holy Spirit helped me to see my need of Jesus as both Saviour and Lord? Throughout the Gospel, Jesus himself is the focal point of attention. John reminds us that one of the ministries of the Holy Spirit is to bear testimony to the Son (15:26). Jesus bears testimony to himself, but his testimony does not stand alone, for the Father, John the Baptist, the Scriptures and his mighty works all bear witness that he is the one who would come from God (5:30-47). I was once approached by an enquirer who had great difficulty with what he called the presumption of Jesus, who always seemed to be drawing attention to himself. I can sympathize with his problem because he had yet to understand that, if Jesus was the only way to God, then it was necessary that he should do so. If this is your difficulty, try to see it like this. During the last war a young lady went to Waterloo station one evening to meet her soldier fiancé', who was arriving on a troop train. There was, of course, a blackout and no bright lights were allowed. Trying to find him in the semi-darkness was almost impossible with thousands of people milling around. So she got the idea of standing on a baggage truck and shining the light of her pencil-beam torch on her face. Then she shouted at the top of her voice, 'David, here I am'.Apart from the amusement, as several Davids approached her with typical British Tommy good humour, the right David found her. There was nothing offensive in the way she drew attention to herself, nor could one find fault with the reason. It was the only way. Similarly, Jesus draws attention to himself as the Saviour of the world, the only way to the Father (14:6). We must therefore come to terms with Jesus saying constantly, in one way or another, 'It is to me you have to come'. This is particularly relevant to our Lord's use of the phrase 'I am', and it is these great claims that lie at the root of much of his teaching in the Gospel. Before we consider them, however, we must give attention to at least two conversations Jesus had, one with Nicodemus and the other with the woman at the well of Sychar, which are recorded in chapters three and four respectively.

HIS TEACHING ABOUT REGENERATION *(3:1-21,31-36)*

This first study in the teaching of Jesus is all about being born again, regeneration, receiving new life through Christ. There is a lot of misunderstanding about the use of phrases such as 'born again', and I have even known sincere Christians to be offended by them. We had been studying this very chapter in one of our own home Bible study groups and one lady present, who was a deeply committed Christian, said, 'There is one thing I don't want to be, and that is "born again'. Of course, the reason she said it was because she did not appreciate its meaning and had been misled by what she called 'the antics of certain people who liked to be known as Born Again Christians'. The truth is that it is impossible to be a Christian without being born again. So let us look at the way in which Jesus unfolded the great doctrine of regeneration to Nicodemus.

Nicodemus the Pharisee

We know three things about Nicodemus. He was a Pharisee (v.1) and therefore, in the best sense of the term, pious. the Pharisees (Separatists) had their origin in the Hasidhim (Pietists) who refused to be influenced by Greek secularism during the second century BC and in consequence established a very precise code of religious behaviour. The problem was that it led to what has been called 'externalism', an outward show of religion without a great deal of spiritual substance. In some it produced mere exhibitionism, which Jesus consistently denounced. Nevertheless they did have some very creditable members such as Paul and Gamaliel. It was to this party that Nicodemus belonged. He is also described as a ruler of the Jews (v.1) and therefore an aristocrat. Finally (v.10), Jesus refers to him as a 'teacher of Israel' from which we deduce that he was a scholar and well versed in Old Testament writings. In spite of these advantages, Nicodemus is quite unable to understand the teaching of Jesus. Several suggestions have been offered as to why he came to Jesus by night. Perhaps he was afraid of criticism from his fellow members of the Sanhedrin. It could have been because it was too difficult to speak with Jesus at any length during the day. The former is generally accepted as the most likely reason but, whichever it was, Nicodemus was a genuine seeker after truth.

The Dilemma that leads to Discovery

Nicodemus was a man deeply troubled by what he had seen and heard. He had evidently been awakened by the 'signs' and had come to recognize that Jesus received his power from God (v.2); but could he possibly be the Messiah who would set up the kingdom so eagerly awaited by the Jews? The fact that Jesus mentions the kingdom of God in his reply suggests that Nicodemus was wondering whether Judaism could ever cradle such a kingdom as Christ taught. It is the same problem that faces the Jew of the twentieth century. The idea was so radical, but his desire to know the truth drove him to seek an answer, and the compelling ministry of Christ drew him to the only place where he could find it. The phrase 'Truly, truly, I say unto you' is rather like Jesus saying 'I know your understanding of Judaism makes it difficult for you Nicodemus, but what I say to you is the truth.'

c) The Discovery that leads to Decision

The word 'kingdom' in the original means 'rule'. Under the Old Testament dispensation, the children of God lived by rules made by God and given through Moses. Under the New Testament dispensation, the children of God live by the Spirit of God who rules from within. It is one thing to live by rule; it is another to experience the kingdom of God, which can only come about when there is a divine renewal. This is the miracle of the new birth of which Jesus now speaks. Every person who would become a true child of God needs to be born again, not of the flesh but of the Spirit. There are three words here all of which must be understood:

The word 'again' in verse 3. The greek *anothen* can mean 'anew', 'from above', 'afresh' or, as Nicodemus' reply in verse 4 indicates, 'a second time'. Certainly a second birth is implied here, but not of the same kind as physical birth.

The word 'water' in verse 4. The whole context suggests this must be understood in conjunction with the baptismal rite of John the Baptist. Still in the Old Testament dispensation, he prepared men for the coming kingdom by baptizing them with water unto repentance. Where there is true repentance, there is forgiveness, and without this repentance we cannot enter into the kingdom. Water is the symbol of the cleansing which follows repentance. The sign must be accompanied by the deed. There is no value in the rite of baptism if it stands alone without the repentance which it represents. When Jesus says (v.5) 'unless one is born of water', he is in fact saying 'unless one repents'. It is the repentance, not the water, which opens the way for forgiveness. Jesus identified himself with John's message of repentance when he allowed himself to be baptised by John in the river Jordan.

The word 'Spirit' in verse 4. The reference here is to the Holy Spirit, and not just to a new kind of inspiration or attitude. Being born of water, repentance with the accompanying rite of baptism, is man's approach to God: being born of the Spirit is God coming to man. How this comes about is beyond man to understand (vv 7-8), but the divine operation is that God by the Holy Spirit brings his own life to repentant man. This is regeneration. But, asks Nicodemus, how can this possibly come about? How can this miracle of grace happen in my own life?(v.9). Not surprisingly, Jesus takes him back to the Old Testament (vv.14-15; see also Numbers 21:5-9). Those who looked upon the serpent were saved from death and their lives were preserved.   Similarly, those who look to Christ crucified are saved from the consequences of their sins, which is death (not physical but spiritual) and receive eternal life. By eternal life we do not mean 'everlasting' in the sense that it goes on for ever. It is the quality of life, not the quantity or duration, that is in mind. The Holy Spirit, who is the agent of the Godhead, brings to the believer the life of God, which cannot be touched by corruption or decay. It is not, therefore, just future, it is now (v.36).

We have no further words from Nicodemus in the narrative but some are bound to be asking the question, why is Jesus' death on the cross set before us as the focal point of belief? It is part of the supplementary nature of the Gospel not to expound in detail much that is found elsewhere in the New Testament.   3:16 has often been hailed as the verse in the Bible most used to bring enquirers into faith. It tells us that to believe in Jesus is the one way we may be freed from the consequences of our sins and receive eternal life. Verses such as 1 Peter 2:24, however, tell us why this is so: 'He himself bore our sins in his body on the tree'. As the hymn puts it, 'In my place condemned he stood'. The heart of the Gospel is that, on the cross, Jesus bore away the sin of the world. The greatest 'hand out' is that by accepting this as God's provision for my salvation and by submitting to Jesus as my Lord, he gives me his own life which is eternal.

The Decision that leads to Discipleship

We are not told of the immediate result of the conversation

between Jesus and Nicodemus but we do meet this inquiring Pharisee twice more in the Gospel, both of which suggest that he became a true disciple. First, we find him sharing the hostility directed at Christ (7:52). The phrase 'Are you from Galilee too?' is a sneering remark and reveals how Nicodemus was prepared to confess his allegiance to Christ. It also indicates that he was increasing in boldness, especially if calling upon the 'Teacher' by night was due to fear of his colleagues in the Sanhedrin. Secondly, we find him serving the needs of Christ (19:38-42). This was an act of unswerving dedication to the Lord, and notice the cost.

Questions for Discussion

1) In verse 5, what is the relationship between being born of water and being born of the Spirit? How does the latter complete and supercede the former?

2) How would you explain 'being born again' to an uninstructed church member?

3) Can you think of situations similar to Nicodemus in 7:52 and 19:38-42, where you might bear testimony to your faith in Christ?

Chapter 8

HIS TEACHING ABOUT LIVING WATER *(4:1-42)*

It is very significant that John follows the subject matter of chapter 3 with that of chapter 4. Having spoken to Nicodemus of the need to be born of 'water' (ch.3), Jesus now offers himself as the Living Water to the woman at the well of Sychar (ch.4). Anybody who has studied the previous chapter will have no difficulty in seeing the connection straight away. Another very interesting link is that the woman of chapter 4 is a splendid example of someone else who came out of darkness into the light and liberty of the Gospel.

Much of our Christian understanding is derived from the conversations which Jesus had with various people. This is mainly because the questions asked are so often the questions we ourselves are asking, though possibly in a different context. Bishop Westcott said, 'John preserves the most universal aspect of Christ's teaching'.

Background to the Occasion

For the origin of the Samaritan schism, read 2 Kings 17:21-34 and note John 4:7-9. As a background to the occasion; it might be helpful to know that the village of Sychar nestles beneath the holy mount of the Samaritan sect, Mount Gerizim. If we were to visit the modern Nablus, ancient Samaria, which the writer has done several times, we would still be able to meet the remnants of the Samaritans. There is a well at Sychar which is extremely deep (v.11), giving authenticity to the story. We shall consider the experiences through which this woman passed under four simple headings.

The Confrontation (vv.7a)

The woman came face to face with Jesus at a time when any thoughts of God or Messiah were farthest from her mind. God often confronts us when we least expect him. I personally was helped into faith when out of the blue I received a letter from my sister, who wrote to me about her own conversion to Christ. St Paul is a typical instance of this (Acts 9:3). One might expect to meet with God in the grand setting of a cathedral or a church service, certainly at an evangelistic meeting or when crying out to him for help in time of trouble, but not when lowering a skin bucket into a well or filling a kettle with water to make a cup of tea, or perhaps watching a ball game. Yet this is often God's way. He confronted some of the disciples at the beginning of a day's work, Bartimaeus as he sat outside the walls of Jericho, and the thief when he was dying on a gibbet, of all places. We must never be surprised if God in Christ should confront us at any time, even at this very moment.

The Conversation (vv.7b-15)

It was not just when he approached her, but the way in which he approached her, which begs our attention. There are three things which can be said about it.

It was *unconventional* (v.7). It began conventionally enough. Jesus was thirsty; she had come to draw water; what could be more natural than for him to ask her for a drink? After all, Abraham's trusted servant had approached Rebecca in exactly the same way (Genesis 24:17-18). The unconventional thing was that he was a Jew but she was a Samaritan (v.9), and who in all oriental history heard of a Jewish man asking a Samaritan woman for a drink (v.10)? Apart from anything else, according to the Jewish laws of purity it was forbidden for a Jew to share a drinking vessel with a Samaritan, and she must have been fully aware of this. The important thing to notice is that Jesus was not bound by convention. This does not mean that he did not respect custom but that he never allowed it to stand in the way of furthering the Gospel. Convention is never so sacrosanct that it cannot be subjected to a greater cause. Take for example his attitude toward the Sabbath, with which we have already become familiar. With Jesus, convention always gave way to spiritual necessity.

It was *radical* (v.14). As far as she was concerned, what Jesus said was a new teaching altogether (v.14). It was radical in so far as he offered what her religion had never taught her to expect. He was, of course, speaking about the effectual working of the Spirit within the life of a believer. Just as water satisfies a thirsting body, so he will quench the longings of a thirsty soul. Following an address on this theme which I had given at a University Christian Union meeting, I was approached by a student who said that his theology had been turned upside-down because he had always understood that the Holy Spirit had been given to him at his baptism through the application of water. By this he meant that the rite itself was sufficient to procure the coming of the Holy Spirit into his life. This is the doctrine of externalism. The need, as we have seen, is for repentance and faith, of which the application of water is an accompanying sign, and it was along these lines that we talked. It was his concluding comment that is relevant to our present study 'this is so radical', he said. The woman found the words of Jesus 'so radical', and many have had to rethink their whole understanding of the Christian Gospel before coming into the experience of which Jesus is speaking here. The radical Jesus was constantly at variance with the religious teaching of his day because so much of it was contrary to the Scriptures. The Pharisees taught that it was sinful to associate with Gentiles and sinners, but Jesus ate and drank with them. They taught that one had to keep the law and the prophets in order to enter the kingdom of heaven, but Jesus said 'No one comes to the Father but by me'. They taught that a man was good when he was religious, but Jesus said that although they might be religious,they were proud and arrogant and therefore guilty before God, and the people of Sodom and Gomorrah had a better chance in the Day of Judgement than they had. There is a hideous emptiness about mere conventional Christianity.

It was *spiritual* (vv.13-15). She was a very earthbound and materialistically minded person, and the spiritual significance of what Jesus said completely escaped her. She had tried most things life had to offer and found them wanting. For her, life had become a ceaseless round of day-to-day routine, part of which was to visit the well, probably several times a day. 'What,never come here again! Sir, give me this water'. And so Jesus sets about telling her how she may receive it.

Her *Conviction* (v.16-18)

The strength of her conviction lies in the fact that she had something she wanted to hide. 'Call your husband', said Jesus. She spoke the truth when she said that she had no husband, but it was only a half truth. She intended to deceive, but could no more fool Jesus than she could fool herself. He lays bare the sordidness of her life. Fact number one about sin is that God knows. So, like many of us when we are under conviction, she changes the subject and tries another tack, seeking to smother her conscience by turning the conversation round to religion (v.20; see footnote on worship.) She was neither the first nor the last to try and hide behind a veneer of religion. I vividly recall once being told quite angrily by a parishioner, 'I believe in God and all that', and this to excuse what was actually a criminal offence. Another accusation against God I have often come across is that he seems to enjoy ferreting out the wickedness in man. God is in fact more like a physician diagnosing a disease which, because of our blindness we cannot,or because of our shame we will not, see. In this manner Jesus approaches the woman. He is saying to her, 'If you want the regenerating, cleansing and refreshing experience of the Holy Spirit, which will be like a well of water springing up within you, then you must first deal with sin in your life and I am the only one who can help you with that.' He reveals himself openly to her as the Messiah (v.26).

Her *Conversion* (vv.28-29)

We have no precise details, only the evidence of her belief. She returns home, leaving her water pot, so great is her haste,and tells everyone about Jesus. The use of the phrase 'many more' in verse 41 indicates that the woman herself had come into a firm faith. It is important to notice in verse 42 that each convert heard for himself or herself. It reminds us that we all need a personal encounter with him, whom they came to see as 'the Saviour of the World'.

Questions for Discussion:

1) In what way would you say God confronts individuals today and how might such a confrontation be recognized?

2) Jesus was a radical teacher. No earthly church is perfect,neither can it claim to hold all the truth. So how can we determine what the truth really is in matters of faith and practice?

3) In what way is Jesus the Saviour of the world?

Footnote on Worship

Read verses 20 to 24. The Samaritans base their teaching on the Pentateuch, the first five books in the Bible. As will have been seen from 2 Kings 17f., the sect was formed at a time when the Israelites of the northern kingdom were scattered throughout the Assyrian empire. When the priest was called to instruct the people of Samaria in the ways of Jehovah, he was at a great disadvantage because the people of the northern kingdom did not have a Davidic dynasty or the tribe of Judah from which the Messiah was to come. Salvation would come from the Jews (v.22). Furthermore, races had so intermingled that there was no way the purity of the Jewish people could be assured. It was largely because of this that the form of Jehovah worship which developed became somewhat syncratistic and impure, because it adopted many customs from foreign religions. This is the main reason why the prophets were so against mixed marriages. In addition, they did not have Jerusalem and the Temple. God had said to Moses, 'There I will meet with you' (hence v.20). So Mount Gerizim had become the holy mount of the Samaritans. But the Jerusalem question was not of the upmost importance for several reasons. The first was because Jesus knew (see Matthew24; Mark 13; Luke 21) that Jerusalem would be destroyed, and then where would one worship Jehovah? There are verses in these chapters which refer to the fall of Jerusalem in AD70 as well as to the end of the age. Secondly, the Temple belonged to the Old Testament era, but the new era had dawned with the coming of Messiah and all that the Temple worship anticipated had come to pass (see v.26). Thirdly, with the coming of the Holy Spirit,true worshippers would gain their inspiration from within. This does not mean that outward symbols are of no value in the New Testament Age and should have no place whatever in the life of the church. On the contrary, Jesus himself instituted symbols in the rites of Holy Communion and Baptism, and where would we be if the symbol of the cross were never to be seen? The final judge of the value and correctness of all worship is that it is inspired by the Holy Spirit combining with our spirits to produce the exaltation of Christ, the Saviour of the World, and that it is in keeping with the Holy Scriptures, the truth.

Question for Discussion

1) How do we account for different forms of worship, and how is it possible that each in their own way could be acceptable to God and beneficial to the worshipper?

Chapter 9

His Teaching about The Bread of Life *(6:22-71)*

It was now 'the next day' following the feeding of the 5,000 and the miracle of the loaves and fishes was uppermost in everybody's mind. The scene was set for some of the most moving words Jesus ever spoke. There is, however, a recurring phrase in the Gospel which demands special attention: the words 'I am'.

I AM.

There are several occasions in the Gospel when John uses 'ego eimi', an emphatic 'I am', coupled with a predicate such as I am 'the Bread of Life'. These predicates are symbolic titles Jesus applied to himself. The origin of the formula is to be found in the Old Testament (Exodus 3:14-16), where God revealed himself to Moses in a manner not previously known to his people (see also Exodus 6:3). Literally, the meaning of the Hebrew is 'I am [for ever] the same'. It relates to the self-existent,timelessness of God and is associated with the sacred name (YHWH) Jehovah. The use of 'ego eimi' by Jesus, placed him on a level with God which would account for the Jews taking up stones to stone him (John 8:58-9). The importance of this is that Jesus said, 'You will die in your sins unless you believe that I am (He)' (8:24), where the 'he', which is added in most versions, is not in the original text. Once again John is offering Jesus to his readers as truly God. Not to believe this carries with it the gravest consequences, 'You will die in your sins'. The implication in the passage before us is that God in Christ is among us as the 'Bread of Life'. This is yet another emphatic claim for our Lord's deity.

Seek first the true Bread *(vv.22-34)*

Jesus perceived that the company had followed him because he had provided loaves for the multitude to eat. Immediately, he draws attention away from something which perishes to something which endures (vv.26-27). We must not long for food which only satisfies bodily needs and has no abiding value, but for spiritual food which produces eternal life and sustains it. If that for which you work only sustains the body, then it is indeed deadly. There is a bread for which a person can work which will nourish the soul unto eternal life, and only the Son of Man (Messianic title) can give this. The 'seal' in verse 27 is a possible reference to the 'signs'. Verse 30 may suggest this, but some prefer the baptism of Jesus. In either case, it is the Father who is announcing our Lord's deity.

The reply they gave to Jesus was typical. 'What must we do?' In other words, what works of the law must we perform to secure a place in the kingdom? I have often found a hint of this necessity to do something at funeral services, when a relative or friend feels the need to speak to the minister about the deceased. It usually comes out like this; 'He was a good man, Vicar. If ever anyone has gone to Heaven, it's him.' The question is, Is anyone ever good enough for God? The only acceptable good work is to 'believe in Him whom the Father has sent' (v.29). Some have difficulty here. It seems unreasonable to them that eternal life should be given just by believing. Surely there must be some achievement or endeavour on the part of the individual? The answer is that good works are the evidence and accompaniment of faith: 'The work of God is that you believe.' I must include part of a paragraph from Hendriksen here. He gives a most helpful illustration in his commentary on the Gospel (John p.232). Salvation, he reminds us, is entirely by grace, which 'does not exclude the idea that man must render to God the work of faith. The roots of a tall oak perform a well-nigh unbelievable amount of work in drawing water and minerals from the soil to serve as nourishment for the tree. Nevertheless, these roots do not themselves produce these necessities but receive them as a gift. Similarly, the work of faith is the work of receiving the gift of God.'

In verse 30, the crowd requested a sign from Jesus; evidently the feeding of the 5,000 had not been sufficient to persuade them. They pointed out that Moses gave his credentials by providing manna in the wilderness (Exodus 16). Our Lord's reply was very straight. He points out that it was not Moses who gave the manna, but His Father, who gives the true bread which comes down from heaven and gives life to the world. Their reply, 'Lord, give us this bread always', indicates how very blind was their blindness. Jesus said (v.35), 'I am the bread of life'.

Coming to Christ and the Promise of Resur-rec-tion *(vv.35-51)*

Five times in this section Jesus emphasizes the need to come to him. I often wonder what some preachers have in mind when they invite members of their congregation to 'come to Jesus'. It is a perfectly sound invitation. After all, Jesus himself, said 'You will not come to me that you might have life' (5:40), but what did he mean? I well remember being approached by a student after a sermon I preached at Cockfosters. He said, 'you have persuaded me of my need to come to Christ, but how do I come?' This is a salutary reminder to all preachers to be explicit! Let me say straight away that coming to Christ is not just an emotional swoon in his direction. Neither is it simply a feeling of love towards him, however desirable and commendable that may be. It is very much more like a person who discovers that in order to know the way to a certain place, he has to go to So and So to find out. This could be accompanied by thankfulness, relief, happiness and great peace of mind, which certainly would be the case if there was confidence as well. Coming to Christ is much more a question of the mind than of the heart. It is truly believing that Jesus both has and is the answer to questions relating to salvation. Yet many refuse to come to him for the solution to life (5:40). The problem the Jews had was they could not bring themselves to believe in the son of Joseph and Mary, whom they knew to be humble folk from Nazareth. How could he possibly have 'come down from heaven' (v.42)? I think it unlikely that anyone would come into faith simply by contemplating our Lord's home background. It is elsewhere we must look for understanding and inspiration. It is not as Jesus the carpenter's son but as the Son of God to whom we must look, for he has the words of eternal life. And if there is to be a focal point for our gaze, then let it be the cross for, as we have already seen, it is here that he bore away the sin that separates us from the Father. The bread which he would give for the life of the world was his own body (v.51b; see also ch.12:32).

The promise to all who believe is that he will raise them up at the last day (vv. 39, 40, 44, 50, 51).

Feeding upon the Son of God *(vv. 52-71)*

This section raises a question which has divided the church for centuries. In what sense does one eat the flesh and drink the blood of the Son of Man (vv.53-6)? Notice that the Jews,characteristically, took Jesus' words literally and regarded this as totally absurd (v.52). Even the disciples found his words hard to swallow (v.60), and so he takes them aside and explains what he means (v.61): 'Supposing you saw the Son of Man ascend into Heaven, how could you possibly eat His flesh and drink His blood physically?' (v.62). Only the Spirit can give life. So we conclude that we partake of Christ in a spiritual and inward manner. But how do we do this? Bishop Westcott, in his commentary on John's Gospel (p112/113), carefully points out that the benefits of 'believing' are the same as 'eating' and 'drinking' (vv.40, 51). He also quotes St Augustine's famous words, 'Believe and thou hast eaten'. By this we understand that when we believe Christ to be the Son of God and accept him as such, and commit ourselves to his revelation of the truth,i.e. his teaching (John 8:51), we do feed upon him and are thereby nourished in our souls unto eternal life.

This is My Body, this is My Blood

What is the link, if there is one, between this chapter and the institution of the Last Supper? Many commentators hold the view that, whereas the synoptics give an historical account of the institution of the Last Supper, John, in chapter 6, provides the theology as a necessary supplement. It highlights the disagreement there is between those who say that the Service of Holy Communion is simply a memorial service, and those who insist that it is very much more. One thing we cannot dismiss is the similar strong language which is used in both instances. 'Take, eat, this is my body', and again, 'Drink...for this is my blood' (Matthew 26:26-8; compare John 6:53, 'Unless you eat the flesh of the Son of Man and drink His blood you have no life in you'). Barrett (p.247), says that the fact that John adds the phrase' and drink his blood (see also v.56), unmistakably points to the Eucharist (Holy Communion Service). Certainly it is an interruption of the 'Bread of Life' theme. The real question,however, is whether we are to accept that this discourse is only to be understood in terms of the Holy Communion? The answer, I believe, has to be 'no', and for several reasons.

1) It is doubtful whether Jesus would give a theological exposition on a sacrament he was yet to institute.

2) In the accounts of the institution of the Lord's Supper there is no mention of eternal life or resurrection which are the main benefits offered in the Bread of Life discourse. The one benefit mentioned is forgiveness, but that is associated with Christ's death and not with partaking of the cup.

3) Nowhere is it suggested that unless you receive Holy Communion you will perish everlastingly, but in the discourse Jesus says emphatically, 'Unless you eat...and drink...you have no life in you'.

4) The virtues of Christ's humanity which bring us into union with the Father are appropriated by believing and receiving, and not by physical eating (v.29).

Does this mean there is no connection at all between the discourse and the Last Supper? No! There are very close connections, but they are related more to the spiritual overtones of the service than to the actual rite itself. As Jesus said,'The flesh [i.e. His Body] is of no avail'. Nothing would be accomplished by actually eating his flesh. In the same way nothing is accomplished simply by eating bread and drinking wine in the sacrament of Holy Communion. Even if it were possible to recreate the elements into the actual body and blood of Christ, the Bible tells us it would profit us nothing, for it is the Spirit who gives life. It does not take a great deal of spiritual insight to see how this is applied to receiving bread and wine in the Eucharist - a good word because it means 'thanksgiving' - where the physical elements are but symbols of the body broken and the life poured out for the sin of the world. To feed on Christ in the heart and not with the mouth, is life indeed.

Questions for Discussion

1) What do you think Jesus meant when He said 'You will die in your sins' *(John 8:24)?*

2) 'We are not saved by works of the law'. -Discuss.

3) Share your experience of how you came to Christ.

4) How would chapter 6 help you in your approach to the Holy Communion service? How important is it, and how often do you think one should attend such a service, and why?

Chapter 10

His Teaching on Being the Light of the World (8:12-59)

The Feast of Tabernacles

Chapters 7 and 8 revolve around the Feast of Tabernacles, one of the most colourful of the Jewish Festivals. It was the occasion when Jesus began his final journey to Jerusalem. At first he was reluctant to reveal himself, for his time had not fully come (7:8-10). John Marsh calls this 'The divine Incognito' (Saint John, page 328). However, in the middle of the Feast he begins teaching in the Temple (7:14). Most of chapter 7 comprises discussions which Jesus had with the Jews about his identity, authority and destiny. Each day during the feast, large numbers of people came with palms and processed round the altar of sacrifice. While this was going on, priests made their way to the Pool of Siloam and filled golden pitchers with water. Passing through the Water Gate they made their way to the Temple site, the people chanting Isaiah 12:3, 'Therefore with joy shall you draw water out of the wells of salvation'. The water was then poured out on the altar as an offering to Jehovah.

The last day of the feast was especially impressive. The people walked round the altar seven times, a crusade of voices ringing out Psalms 113-8. It was in the midst of such fervour and enthusiasm that a solitary figure stood and cried out: 'If any one thirst, let him come to me and drink. He who believes in Me, as the Scripture has said, out of his heart shall flow rivers of living water' (vv.37-8). We have studied enough of the Gospel already to realise what an impact this must have made on the assembled company. Here was Jesus, bursting upon the scene, and offering himself once again as the one who had come from God. The words remind us of his conversation with the woman at the well in chapter 4. The evangelist's comment in verse 39 is an exposition of the previous verse.

The Light of the World

Chapter 8 continues the emphasis on the person and authority of Jesus. There are very few commentators who do not accept that 8:12f is the natural continuation of the controversy begun in the previous chapter. Following the incident of the woman taken in adultery, which is not included in some ancient authorities and is therefore added as a footnote in some editions of the Bible (vv.1-11), we have the second of the great 'I am' sayings of Jesus: 'I am the light of the world' (v.12). Unlike the discourse on 'the Bread of Life', there is no prolonged statement in the Gospel on the theme of Jesus being Light, although it is referred to some twenty times. This being the case, we shall draw together the various passages where Jesus is symbolized by Light and seek to bring into perspective the implications. The first thing we are told is that Jesus came into the world as Light. It is a claim which he made for himself (8:12, 9:5), and it is an attribute ascribed to him by John in the Prologue to the Gospel (1:4,7-9).

If the ceremony of pouring out the water, mentioned above, prompted Jesus to cry out, 'If anyone thirst let him come to me and drink', it is more than likely that the ceremony of lighting the candlesticks in the Court of the Women inspired the proclamation 'I am the light of the world'. For full details of this ceremony the research student may care to read Sukkah, 5:2-4, where it is fully described. The Light was only in the world temporarily (10:35), but would live on in his disciples who become 'sons of light' (12:36; see also Matt.5:14 where, in the Sermon on the Mount, Jesus calls his disciples 'lights of the world' Lesser lights, no doubt, but lights nevertheless).

Light described as the Way, the Truth and the Life

It is very difficult to describe light. Unlike most objects, which have dimensions and appearance, light has no shape and can only be measured by the human eye in relation to its intensity and colour. The scientist can describe it in terms of light waves and so on, but to most of us it is best understood by its functions and the use to which it is put. There are three main functions of light. It leads, it illuminates, and it promotes life. In the Gospel we see Jesus as Light functioning in all three ways. This is clearly illustrated in yet another well known 'I am' passage where he said of himself 'I am the Way, the Truth, and the Life' (14:6). We shall consider the work of Jesus as Light under these three headings:

As Light, Jesus leads *(8:12a)* - *'He who follows Me'*.

He is the Way. There are thousands of ways in which light is used to lead people from one place to another. One of my passions is for sailing, which provides a good illustration of what I have in mind. Imagine that you are on the high seas at night time and that you are trying to make harbour. True, you have your chart and compass, but there is one thing you are on the watch for all the time, and that is the harbour lights to lead you home. As Light, Jesus brings us home to the Father (14:6). He is the only way.

As Light, Jesus illuminates *(8:12b)* - *'shall not walk in darkness'*.

He is the Truth. Often, when one is trying to explain something, someone will say, 'Oh, I see what you mean'. As light, Jesus helps us to see the Truth. i.e, the truth about God, about himself and the Holy Spirit' about the way of salvation, and about all else relating to the things we need to know concerning eternal life (see 17:6-8,17). This is another momentous revelation of the deity of Christ, because 'Truth' is an absolute, and absolutes belong to God alone. You cannot be more truthful than true (see also 8:31-32, 39-51).

As Light, Jesus promotes Life *(8:12c)* *'but will have the light of life.*

He is the Life. As 'the Life' Jesus is the Life-giver, and what he gives is his own life which is eternal. Where there is no light there is no life. In Genesis 1:3 we learn that the very first thing

God created was light. I remember hearing an eminent scientist speaking on the radio about the origin of life, and I have never forgotten his concluding sentence. He said,'Whatever view we may have of the creation narratives in the Old Testament, there is one fact with which we cannot argue. Before there was any life on the universe, there had to be light'. Jesus comes among us as light, the life-giver 1:4, 'In him was life and the life was the light of men. See also 1:9.

Reaction to the Light

Put simply, 'men loved darkness rather than light because their deeds were evil' *(3:19-20)*. Because of its sinful nature, humankind is more at home in the darkness of ignorance and unbelief than in the light of the Gospel, which it finds an embarrassment. It is for this very reason that an attempt was made to put out the Light by crucifying the Son of God. That Light, however, was not, nor ever will be, put out. 'The darkness has not overcome it' (1:5). There have always been, and always will be, those who walk in the light (11:9). The theme of walking in the Light is very pronounced in John's first epistle (1.John 1:5-9), where he shows very simply how one may walk out of darkness and into the light. The need is to confess our sins, that we might be forgiven and experience his cleansing. Then we can continue walking in the light and enjoy a new kind of oneness, first with the Father and then with one another. There is a very supportive passage in 1 Peter 2:9-10.

Questions for Discussion

1.) How would you explain the experience 'out of his heart shall flow rivers of living water?.

2.) Can you agree among yourselves as to the meaning of 'I

am the Way, the Truth, and the Life'?

3.) The normal human experience of walking in the daytime is so much more satisfying than walking in darkness. Why is it that so many prefer to walk in spiritual darkness? Using the passages mentioned above, how would you set about explaining the way to discover the Light and then to encourage an unbeliever to walk in it?

Chapter 11

His Teaching about the Good Shepherd (10:1-30)

The Door of the Sheep

There are two 'I am' passages in this chapter. The first is in verses 1-10, the key phrase of which is 'I am the door of the sheep'(vv.7 and 9). This is a very colourful way of saying that 'No one can enter the kingdom of heaven but by me'. The imagery does not call for any vivid description, as the picture is so simple and clear. When I was at Sunday School I remember my teacher explaining how sheep were gathered into the fold at night and how the shepherd would lie across the entrance. He did this to protect them and ensure that no strange sheep would enter the pen. Later, when I visited the Holy Land, I actually witnessed this taking place and the childhood vision came to life, except that the pen was constructed of corrugated iron sheets, which somewhat took the romance out of the picture I had conjured up in my childhood mind. Remember, Jesus is speaking to the Pharisees (9:400, who found his words very difficult to understand (v.6). Had they been ready to accept him as the long awaited Messiah, they would have had no such difficulty.

You cannot take the kingdom by storm or stealth (v.1). You have to be led by the Shepherd himself, who has gained an entrance into the kingdom because his life alone is wholly acceptable to the Father (v.2-3a). The sheep know him intimately and they follow him wherever he goes. Just as a door is the only way into a room so the Shepherd is the only way by which the flock enters into the fold. The theme is developed in verses 7-9, the emphasis being that Jesus is the only way into the kingdom.

We do well to think carefully about the relationship and communication the sheep enjoy with the Shepherd (vv.3-4). Notice also the discernment which is more than hinted at in verse5.

The Good Shepherd

The phrase 'I am the Good Shepherd ' is probably one of the best known of all in the Bible. Most people instinctively associate it with the Shepherd Psalm (Psalm 23), but in fact John 10 is much more related to another Old Testament passage which Jesus clearly had in mind when he embarked on this discourse. The passage is Ezekiel 34, and we need to keep the chapter in front of us as we proceed with our study. It is concerned with God's indictment of the spiritual leaders of Israel, whom he likens to evil shepherds whose chief interest is not the sheep but themselves (vv.1-6). In consequence he sets his face against the shepherds of Israel and declares that he himself would be Shepherd to his flock (vv.7-10). We will consider the chapter under three headings:

The person of the Shepherd

Once again John loses no opportunity to stress the deity of Christ. He does so in two ways by using the phrase 'I am the Good Shepherd'.

The use of the words 'I am'. We have already seen that by using these words, the divine title, Jesus was making his claim to deity, and that the Jews, being well aware of the significance of this, took up stones to stone him because to them it was blasphemy of the worst kind (compare John 8:58-9 with10:31-3).

The use of the word 'shepherd'. The concept of God as 'shepherd' is constant to the Jewish mind. David used the imagery long before God himself expounded on the theme through his servant Ezekiel. A close look into Ezekiel 34 will emphasize this. It was as though Jesus was saying 'You remember how God promised that he would be a fair shepherd to his sheep. I am that Good Shepherd now come among you.'

The *performance* of the Shepherd

We would not do justice to the discourse unless we were to embark upon a comparison between Ezekiel 34 and John 10. First, however, we must take a look at the word 'good'. Jesus does not use the common word for good, *'agathos'* which means good in the sense of being morally upright as opposed to being bad. That is the word used in Luke 18:18-19, when Jesus said to the rich young ruler, 'there is no one who is good except God'. This in itself was a claim to deity which Jesus made by not denying his total goodness. In all fairness to the text, however, we have to say that it is not the word Jesus uses in John 10. The word he uses here is *'kalos'* which should be interpreted as fair, lovely, or even beautiful. The picture it brings before us belongs to the genius of the wonderful language of the New Testament. As a shepherd, Jesus is perfect to the extent of being attractively so. He stands before his sheep, the realization of everything the word shepherd means, set forth in such a manner as to be infinitely lovely, perfectly fair, and thoroughly dependable. Is that how we see Jesus?

There are four parallels in the two chapters in question which we should observe:

Jesus is a *Saving* Shepherd *(Ezekiel 34:22, John 10:11)*.

Notice the deliberateness of our Lord's sacrifice in John 10:15b,17-18. It sets forth the purpose of his coming into the world. This, of course, is not a theme peculiar to John. It is an overwhelming theme of the New Testament that Jesus did not come into the world to be served just because he was God, but to serve the world at the deepest level of its need in a way that only God could. For instance, the key verse of Mark's Gospel is10:45, 'The Son of Man came not to be served but to serve and to give his life a ransom for many'. He serves by saving his sheep from the consequences of the sin that separates them from God. He carries it away in his own body on the cross, thus bringing about a reconciliation with the Father. Paul puts it so directly when he writes, 'We were reconciled to God by the death of his Son' (Romans 5:10). How does this come about? Peter tells us, 'He bore our sins in his body on the tree (cross)' (1Pet.2:24). The idea of a shepherd dying to save his sheep may not appeal very much to us in the West in the twentieth century, but it would have been a very powerful imagery to those of our Lord's time in the Middle East.

Jesus is a *Securing* Shepherd (Ezekiel 34:28; John 10:27-8).

This stresses the confidence we should have in his saving work. One of the most important doctrines of the Christian faith is that of assurance. We may be unreservedly confident in the inheritance we have in Christ. One does, however, meet quite a number of Christians who do not have any such assurance. They cling to a weak hope that perhaps they might be children of God and one day, if things go right, they will, as John puts it in chapter 14:3, be with Jesus where he is in heaven. To my deep sorrow I once heard the leader of one of our Christian denominations say, when asked what his main aim in life was, 'My main aim is to be found worthy to be numbered among the children of God in his kingdom'. Surely none of us is worthy of the kingdom of God, and the only hope we have of being accepted in Christ is because he has taken away our sins and clothed us with his own righteousness. It is because of this that he is able to present us faultless before the presence of God (Jude 24). If we had to depend upon our own righteous achievements to be regarded by God as worthy to be one of his children, then we would indeed have cause for doubt, but the beauty of the Christian Faith is that we do not. We depend entirely upon his grace alone to save us (Eph.2:8-10). This great truth has never been better expressed than in the words of Toplady's majestic hymn, 'Rock of Ages':

Not the labours of my hands
Can fulfil Thy law's demands;
Could my zeal no respite know,
Could my tears for ever flow,
All for sin could not atone,
Thou must save, and Thou alone.

Jesus is a *Sustaining* Shepherd. *(Ezekiel 34:14 John 10:16)*.

The word *'agagein'* (John 10:16) in the original is usually translated 'to bring'. Literally the word means 'to lead', and within the context of the chapter it has the idea of taking on the responsibility for leading or bringing the sheep home. It is not only concerned with the arrival but also the journey. The Shepherd absolves the sheep from all anxiety. This care and attention which the Shepherd has for the sheep is one of the most common aspects of his work as a shepherd. See not only Ezekiel 34:14 but also Isaiah 40:11, 'He will feed his flock like a shepherd', and Psalm 23 where the thought of sustaining the sheep is uppermost.

iv) Jesus is a Seeking Shepherd *(Ezekiel 34:11-12,16; John 10:27)*

This is more apparent in Ezekiel than in John, but the spirit of the Old Testament chapter has to be kept very much to the fore when reading the discourse on the Good Shepherd. In verse 3 he calls his sheep and they hear his voice (see also v.27). It would be very easy at this juncture to become involved in the controversial doctrine known as effectual calling, i.e. the extent to which, if at all, a person has the freedom to refuse to respond to such a call. It is very closely associated with the doctrines of predestination and divine sovereignty. I am deliberately avoiding such a temptation because I think a subject of such magnitude demands more space than is justified here. I would, however, commend

Evangelism and the Sovreignty of God, by Dr. J.I.Packer, for some introductory reading on the subject. Whatever the ology lies behind it, one thing is certain: God in Christ, that great Shepherd of the sheep, is seeking his church and we, as individuals, having heard his call, need to make that personal response and rise up to follow him as the disciples did long ago by the shores of Galilee (Matt.4:19).

The persecution of the Shepherd *(vv.31-4)*

This is not the first time the Jews took up stones to stone him because he made claims to deity. (You have probably noticed consistently Jesus not only made such a claim but was also understood to have made it. It is very difficult to understand how Jehovah's Witnesses and others still insist that nowhere did Jesus say that he was God.) The difficulty of this section is understanding the meaning of 'I said, you are god's' (v.34), and why Jesus uses this particular quotation from Psalm 82:6.

i) Notice the two titles given to wayward Israel in the psalm: 'gods' and 'sons of the Most High'. You will see by reading the whole psalm that the psalmist is referring to Israel's exalted position as the redeemed children of God. The very fact that they were wayward excludes them from deity. Jesus is not confusing them with God. God alone is God (v.1).

ii) In the New Testament the redeemed are the children of God (see 1:12 and compare Gal.4:5,7 and Rom.8:15,17,23).

iii) What Jesus is actually doing in verse 34 is challenging the Jews to face up to facts. Are they going to stone him for his use of words, or because of his works (see v.36)? If it is for his words, then what about Psalm 82:6? If it is for his works, then let them be the judges (vv.37-8). In other words, 'Let my works bear testimony to the truth and stone me if you dare!'

Questions for Discussion

1) Why did the Jews find it difficult to understand the words of Jesus in verses 1-5 and how might you explain their meaning?

2) In what ways does the Shepherd serve the sheep? Can you think of instances in the Gospel narratives which illustrate this?

3) In the light of vv.27-8, discuss the following question: Was Paul being presumptious in 2 Timothy 1:12?

4) Verse 42 says that 'many believed in him there'. What evidences of belief are suggested in the chapter?

5) If you have time as a group, can you agree on the meaning of verses 31-9?

CHAPTER 12

HIS TEACHING ABOUT RESURRECTION *(11:24-6)*

Because the resurrection is such an important doctrine and so central to the message of the early church, it would seem profitable for us to take a wider view of the subject than we have given to other themes in this book. We shall go beyond the teaching of Jesus and consider an introduction to the whole question. References which Jesus makes to the resurrection are spread throughout the Gospel. Nowhere does he unfold the nature of it, nor does he seek to justify belief in it. The one thing he does do is accept it. For a developed Christian teaching, we have to go to the apostles.

There is a Resurrection.

This is a bold and stark statement but it is where Jesus stood. He believed in it (John 5:25-9). But not all did. The Pharisees did, but their belief was not well defined. The Sadducees did not, and were prepared to argue their case (Matt.22:23f; Acts 23:8). Paul was mocked because of his belief in it (Acts 17:32), whilst Hymenaeus and Philetus held strange views concerning it (2 Tim.2:18). The resurrection had its opponents in the Early Church as well. Celcus, late second century, made the resurrection a butt of ridicule and the Gnostics, who regarded all matter as evil, refuted it. It had its champions, however. Among the greatest was Origen, early third century, whose massive treatise on Christian theology helped to preserve the doctrine, which has always been well established in the ancient Christian creeds, notably the Apostle's, the Nicene and the Athanasian.

The Resurrection in the Old Testament

There is no clearly formed statement in the Old Testament but Jesus found it implied in Exodus 3:6, 'I am the God of your fathers. The God of Abraham, Isaac and Jacob'. He referred to this passage during the controversy he had with the Sadducees (Matt.22:29-32). The writer to the Hebrews intimates that the patriarchs looked forward to the resurrection long before the Exile (Heb.11:10,13-16,19). The resurrection idea is also very strong in the Psalms: 'God will ransom my soul from the power of Sheol, for he will receive me' (Ps.49:15). Perhaps one of the best known Old Testament references, however, is in Job 19:25-27: 'I know that my Redeemer lives ... then without my flesh I shall see God'. There is one passage from Daniel which Jesus may well have had in mind when he spoke the words of John 5:25-9: 'Many of those who sleep in the dust of the earth shall awake, some to everlasting life, and some to shame and everlasting contempt' (Dan.12:2).

It is difficult to appreciate fully what was in the mind of the Old Testament writers except to say that a firm, if undefined, belief in the resurrection is very evident.

The Resurrection in the New Testament

When we come to the New Testament we are on much surer ground, because it was during the time of Christ and immediately following that the doctrine of the resurrection was fully developed. The bedrock of Christian belief is the resurrection of Jesus, what he has to say about it, and the statements of the apostles who were the interpreters of Christ's teaching. So we have three main sources:

The resurrection appearances, which are recorded in all four Gospels and the Acts of the Apostles (Matt.28, Mark 16, Luke24, John 20-21, Acts 1:1-9).

The teaching of Jesus which, apart from the accounts of the conflict he had with the Sadducees recorded in Matthew 22:29-

32,Mark 12:18-27 and Luke 20:27-38, is to be found entirely in St John's Gospel. The relevant passages are John 5:25-29,11:24-26, 14:1-3 and 17:24.

The main passages recording the apostolic testimony, which are 1 Corinthians 15, 1 Thesssalonians 4:13-16, 2 Corinthians5:1-10 and Revelations 20:4-6,13. There are other verses to which we shall refer as we proceed, but we shall avoid being side-tracked into the meaning of many obscure passages to be found in the Book of Revelation. For further reading on the subject of Revelation, may I refer the reader to More than Conquerors by William Hendriksen and a more recent commentary on the Apocalypse by Philip E. Hughes.

There is a theological point which should also be made, namely that the resurrection is the work of the Triune God: Father, Son and Holy Spirit. It is the Father's work (Matt. 22:29 note the context, John 5:21, 2 Cor.1:9).

It is the Son's work (John 5:21; 6:38-40).

It is the Holy Spirit's work (Romans 8:11).

The bodily nature of the Resurrection
There is obviously a limit to what we can know and understand, and we all too easily fall into the temptation of putting heavenly concepts into earthly moulds. Of all the doctrines, that of the resurrection is most vulnerable to this kind of treatment. I must emphasize that it is neither scriptural no rational to assume that the 'body' of the resurrection is identical to our earthly bodies. This puzzled Christians at Corinth: 'How are the dead raised and with what kind of body do they come?' (1Cor.15:35). Paul answers with the illustration of a kernel (vv.37f.) and from it deduces that, in the resurrection,what is laid to the ground is perishable, sinful, with human limitations and purely physical, but the resurrection body is imperishable, redeemed, without limitations and spiritual, i.e.of the heavenly nature (vv.42-6).

Having said this, all the major creeds include the words 'I believe in the resurrection of the body'. The Westminster Confession elaborates a little and states, 'The very same bodies that are buried in the earth shall be raised and reunited to their souls, their identity preserved, although their qualities will be changed'. This really is a restatement of what we read in the New Testament and there it has to rest. Only a foolish person would go on to elucidate further upon the nature of the resurrection body. All we can say is that it will be a 'spiritual body'. The use of the word 'spirit' in Scripture is not meant to convey a spooky, Marley's ghost, sort of idea - far from it. By its use we mean other worldly, in the sense that God is spirit and therefore it is of the nature of God. We can substitute the word 'heavenly', but it has to be very substantial. All this is concluded from the passages which show our resurrection to be like that of Christ's, the first fruit of all who sleep (1Cor.15:20,23). He is the first of many of th same kind, and in a mysterious way carried humanity into glory. Other passages which should be considered are (Colossians 1:18,Revelation 1:5, both of which speak of Christ as 'the first born of the dead'; Philippians 3:21 'He will change this body of our low estate to be made like unto His glorified body'; Romans 8:11'He will give life unto our mortal body' and, of course, Romans 8:23 'We wait for the adoption of sons, the redemption of our bodies'.

It is significant that, after his resurrection, Jesus identified himself to his disciples through his glorified body, in the garden, in the Upper Room, on the Damascus Road, by the Sea of Galilee and on the Mount of Olives. Anyone wishing to pursue this fascinating theme will find it well discussed in The Confession of Faith by A.A.Hodge and in any reputable book of systematic theology, e.g. Berkhof.

Our Lord's teaching on the Resurrection in John
i) Those who hear and receive his words will come forth to the resurrection of life (5:24-29a; compare 6:39-40,44,47,51 and 11:26). There are two conditions of eternal life: hearing and receiving (v.24). Eternal life is not future but present, in the sense that it is. It is the life of God given to those who 'heed' his words (see 10:16). Those who have received him are no longer under judgement and will come forth to the resurrection of life, i.e. the new life in Christ, and he will raise them up at the last day (6:39,44,54). Westcott reminds us that the doctrine of eternal life makes the resurrection both necessary and obvious (Commentary on John, p103). The phrase 'those who have done good' (v.29) does not infer that a person can achieve the resurrection by a virtuous life. To hear and receive is to do good. A virtuous life may be the evidence of believing, but nobody can attain everlasting life by his own endeavours (see Eph.2:9).

ii) Those who do not receive his words will come forth to the resurrection of condemnation *(5:28-29)*.
This is an adverse judgement which true believers escape because they already possess eternal life (see 3:18-19). There are two levels of judgement, just as there are two levels of eternal life - present and future. Those who are in unbelief are already under judgement, but to die in unbelief is to face a final judgement at the last day (12:48). What the condemnation will bring, John does not tell us in his Gospel. The phrase 'the hour is coming and now is' (5:25), suggests a continuation of the existing situation. To be under judgement then, would mean that a present separation from the Father would continue into eternity. Chapter 17:24 would certainly suggest this. I once heard Brother Edward put it like this: 'Just as a shell leaves the gun barrel and continues in the direction in which it is pointing, so to die unrepentant and thus separated from the life of God means an eternity without him and with no hope of repentance.' We must get away from the

idea that 'judgement' is God waiting for the last day to punish everyone who refuses to accept Jesus as Saviour and Lord. Jesus taught that it is more like a person shut up in a dark cell, although the door is not locked and he need not stay there (Chapter 10:9-10; 11:25). Jesus is the door through which we can pass into the glorious liberty of the children of God. This is daylight indeed (see chapter 3:18-19)!

iii) The joy of Heaven will be to spend eternity with *Christ (14:1-3, 17:24*; see also *Rev.21:22-23). I trust the reader is noticing the many occasions when the thought of believing comes into our Lord's teaching. Let us continue to keep chapter 20:31in mind. Not only the miracles 'signs', but our Lord's teaching also, is intended to bring each of us in turn into faith. Here we are encouraged to heed his words if we would be with him in the Father's presence. There is a monumental amount of discussion as to the meaning of the word 'monai'- rooms, dwelling-places, abodes,- etc. but at the end of the day virtually every commentator of note settles for 'where God is'. Westcott calls it 'The spiritual and eternal antitype of the transitory temple'.One of the most moving passages to come from the pen of the apostle John is on this very theme (Rev.21:1-4). Notice in John17:24 that the redeemed are the Father's gift to the Son. This suggests that it will not only be our joy to be with him but that it will be his joy to welcome us as his own in a very special way.

iv) Jesus himself will be the instrument of resurrection *(5:21,6:40).*
This was mentioned earlier but there is one further thought from George Hutcheson, a Seventeenth century writer of the Puritan school: 'The grave doth not make void his interest,nor cause his affection to cease' (John's Gospel p117). It reminds us of Matheson's beautiful hymn, 'O Love that will not let me go'.

Questions for discussion.

1. Why do you think there is so little about the resurrection in the Old Testament?

2. 'I believe in the resurrection of the body'. All the major creeds contain these words. Explain what you understand them to mean to a neighbour who is interested but not convinced. What Scriptures would you use?

3. Discuss the two conditions, or states, of eternal life and judgement, i.e. a present reality and a future hope. What has God done, and what must be our response, in order that we can pass from death to life?

CHAPTER 13

HIS TEACHING ABOUT THE TRUE VINE, *(15:1-17)*

You will see from the 'Analysis of the Gospel' that we are now in the Upper Room. Chapters 13 to 17 comprise the longest of our Lord's conversations with the disciples, and the phrase 'I am the True Vine' is the last of the great 'I am' passages. It comes right in the heart of the discourse and is, in fact, the only 'I am' which is solely for the disciples' benefit. The teaching in these chapters is intensive and every Christian should become thoroughly familiar with their content.

Judas, that dark blot on the feast of charity, had already left the upper room (13:30), and Jesus, knowing that the die of crucifixion was to be cast in the betrayal, turns to his disciples and announces that the hour of his glory had come. What the disciples made of it at the time we can only surmise but one thing is for sure, they knew that whatever it was that was going to happen was about to take place. The atmosphere must have been very tense and full of expectancy. They would have been highly receptive to every word spoken and responsive to every command. Was he going to stride out into the city and claim his earthly throne? Would he use his exceptional powers to impose his authority over the Romans and gather all Israel about him? Would they suddenly find themselves rulers over Israel within the next twenty four hours? No wonder Peter, impatient as ever, comes out with 'Where are you going?', 'Why can't I come with you now? I will lay down my life for you!' (13:36-7). Unlike the disciples, we are able to look back and with hind-sight understand most of what Jesus was saying. I say 'most', because who can fully plumb the true depths of his words? Far from unfolding plans to take over Jerusalem by divine force, he begins to talk to them about troubles that were to come upon them, about loving one another, and about obedience which would signify their true love for him. He promises that he will not leave them in the lurch and will send one who will be a counsellor, while he himself will return and somehow inspire them with his inner presence (ch. 14).

At this point, Jesus makes as though He is about to leave (14:31), when he launches into yet another theme, 'I am the True Vine...' (15:1-17). I have often wondered whether the look of incredulity that must have come over the disciples' faces when he spoke the words of 14:15-20, gave rise to this beautiful picture of the branch drawing its very life from the vine. One can hear the disciples saying to one another' 'What is all this about a counsellor being in us, and that he, the teacher, will be in us too? What is He saying? (It is all rather rather like 16:16-18.) In the next chapter we shall consider his teaching on the Holy Spirit in more detail, but always remember that the Trinity works in unity. I have ventured to include at the end of this volume a list of the works equally attributed to Father, Son and Holy Spirit, to indicate the extent to which the Bible shows the persons of the Trinity working together.

The Parable of the Vine,*v.1-6.* This is an image which would not have been unfamiliar to the disciples. The Father is the vine-dresser and naturally desires pleasure in the vine. Jesus himself is the true vine, i.e. the main vine from which all the branches derive their life and strength (v.1). Grades of branches are mentioned. There are those which bear no fruit. These are gathered together and burned. Other branches bear a little fruit, and these are pruned in order that they may bear more fruit until they reach the point where the fruit is abundant (v.5, 'much fruit').

It has been said that what we have here is an allegory rather than a parable, i.e. the story has many aspects, each of which contains a spiritual truth. If you like, we have a lot of parables put together. Nevertheless, there is an overriding lesson which super-imposes itself upon all others: namely, it is the Father's will that we should bear much fruit and the only way to achieve this is to abide in Christ. It is this positive thought which must prevail when we conclude our study of the passage. This does not mean that we can overlook certain questions, such as: Of whom was Jesus thinking when he spoke of branches that bore no fruit? To what virtues does the word 'fruit' refer? How does the Father prune the branch-es, and what does it mean to abide?

The True Vine.v 1. This is the seventh of the great 'I am' phrases in the Gospel where the personal pronoun is emphatic (*egoeimi*) and the verb is followed by a predicate. The others are 6:48, 8:12, 10:9, 10:11, 11:25, 14:6. We have already noticed earlier in this book that such a usage has an important bearing upon the claims Jesus made to deity because of its association with the divine Name [chapter 9 par. a)] It is particularly so in this instance because, elsewhere in the Bible, Old and New Testaments, the image of the vine is generally applied to Israel (Isaiah 5:1-7; Jer. 2:21; Ezek. 15:1-8, 19:10-14; Psalm 80:9-16;Mark 12:1-9; Matt. 20:1-16, 21:28-32; Luke 13:6-9). Here, Jesus deliberately applies the image to himself. He does not say 'I am like a vine in the sense that it is a picture of me' but 'I myself am the real vine'. It is in me that all the branches are sustained, and by me they bear fruit - a divine function if ever there was one. Again John loses no opportu-nity to stress the divine nature of Jesus. He is truly God.

The branch that bears no fruit, v.2a,6. You will notice that both the allegory and the interpretation are given. The questions posed are, 'Who do the fruitless branches represent ,and what are we to understand by the burning? Two suggestions regarding the fruitless branches are offered by most commentators. It could be the Jews, who are spoken of as branches in Romans 11:17f (see also Matt. 15:13, 21:41). It does, however, seem much more likely to have meant apostate Christians of whom Judas may be seen as a ready and recent example. The words 'of mine' (v.2), would suggest this as the most likely interpretation. From these words of Jesus we have in mind those who only make a pretence at being Christians and who bear no evidence in their lives that they are true believers. They are dead wood and only fit for burning. However, we must always be careful not to push an illustration too far. There is no suggestion of hell fire in verse 6, as in Dante's Inferno. What is suggested is rejection, then an ongoing dissipation of any appearance of allegiance to Christ, followed by a gathering together of all useless branches, as in Matthew 13:30, ready for the ultimate rejection in judgement as referred to in the previous chapter (comment on 5:28-9). The mention of fire could be understood in the sense that Jesus was simply describing the normal custom, which was to burn useless vine branches (see also Matt. 13:41). Some readers may wish to take a more literal view of this and associate it with the everlasting banishment mentioned in Rev.20:10,14-15. The problem with taking too literal a view is that fire destroys finally and for ever, and annihilation is the consequence. Rev.20:10, however, rejects this by showing the judgement is, for those judged, an eternally conscious state: 'They will be tormented day and night for ever and ever'.

The fruit of the Vine. Jesus had already introduced the theme of the Holy Spirit (14:16), and in a short while would be unfolding his work as Counsellor. It is not unreasonable, therefore, to assume that Jesus had the fruits of the Spirit in mind (see Gal.5:22-3). It is a matter of living the Christ-life, with perhaps an emphasis on the mutual love one Christian should have for another (v.12). It is important at this juncture for the student to consider these graces in turn and engage in a measure of self-examination. Morbid introspection is never helpful, but honest appraisal is a road along which we all need to travel in order to promote spiritual growth. We will leave the question of what these spiritual graces are for group discussion.

Pruning the branches v.2. We must notice two things before considering how God prunes. The first is that the Father does the pruning. The pruning process may be a little painful at times but it is not necessarily so. It is done by the master vine-dresser, who is thoroughly skilled in the management of the branches. Secondly, it is done in order to produce an abundance of fruit for the pleasure of the vine-dresser and to the praise of his glory. The pruning process is therefore an operation which we should welcome. How then does God prune the branches? Consider just three ways, although many more could be suggested:

    i)   **By chastening** *(Heb.12:5-6).*
    ii)   **By testing**   *(Gen.22:1).*
    iii) **By withholding.** *(Rom.8:25)*

Abiding in the Vine. I have often been asked, What is the difference between 'Christ in me' and 'me in Christ'? Swabbing the decks when sailing can be fun. You tie a warp (line) to a bucket handle and throw the bucket overboard in order to fill it with sea water before swilling it over the deck. Now, when the bucket is immersed in the water, is the water in the bucket or is the bucket in the water? The obvious answer is 'both'. You cannot have one without the other. So it is with our being in Christ and Christ being in us. Being 'in Christ' is relative to our status as Christians. We are part of the Body Eternal, and it is by his righteousness that we shall be saved. Because we are in him, he can present us faultless to the Father (his faultlessness, not ours). It is made possible because we have received Christ into our lives by faith. This is the 'Christ in us' which Paul tells us is 'the hope of glory' (Col.1:27). This is regeneration. It is the very Life of the Eternal which has come to us in Christ. His presence in power within us enables us to achieve things spiritual which otherwise would be impossible. This is a section where a simple verse by verse explanation would be of most help to us.

verse 3. The disciples had already been cleansed (13:1-15). 'By the word...spoken' means that they had received the revelation which had come by Christ. Barrett speaks of it as 'the whole loving service of Jesus to men, culminating in his death' (Commentary on John p.395). It is the word of salvation which came with Christ.

verse 4. To abide in Christ is to remain obedient to his world which is kept out of love for him and for no other reason (see vv.7 and 10, also chapter 14 verse 15).

verse 5. It is in abiding in this way that the fruit of Christlikeness is developed, and the more we abide, so the more like him we become.

verse 6. A fruitless life is evidence that the person is not abiding. Put positively, that person is disobedient.

verse 7. When a truly obedient Christian prays, it is always according to the will of his Father, who will be glorified in the answer (v.8). Such a person only seeks to honour Christ through his prayers. They are free from any selfish wish. To pray outside of the Father's will would be through innocence or ignorance. Pruning would then become part of the maturing process.

verse 8. A truly Christian life is proof to the world of the genuineness of faith.

verses 9 and 10. Abiding cultivates the two-way love-relationship which exists between Christ and his true disciples and is already an integral part of that which exists within the Trinity.

verse 11. Abiding is also the secret of fullness of joy. There is a lot of artificial joy in the Christian church today. One way to distinguish between what is real and what is unreal is to mark the measure of obedience. By this I am not suggesting that we should be judging the level of genuineness in others. The intention is that we should be looking at ourselves.

verses 16 and 17 speak for themselves and re-emphasise several thoughts mentioned above. Notice that they do end on a word of command.

Questions for Discussion.

1.) How would you describe the fruit of the Spirit in Galations 5:22-3? In other words, what do you understand by love, joy, peace etc?

2.) How does God prune by chastening, testing and withholding?

3.) Discuss verse 7 and compare Mark.11:24-5. Can you detect a link between forgiving one another, keeping God's law, abiding, and effective prayer?

CHAPTER 14

THE HOLY SPIRIT IN THE GOSPEL

'The Doctrine of the Holy Spirit by George Smeaton provides the best practical teaching on the subject I know', wrote Dr Martyn Lloyd-Jones. The publishers are the Banner of Truth Trust, and it is a book I would recommend every christian to have on the bookshelf. Why do I mention this? Because one chapter on the subject, even if limited to what is written in John's Gospel, will ensure very inadequate treatment of the theme. What John writes, however, is of such importance we must give it our attention.

There are few references to the Holy Spirit in the synoptics compared to those which we find in John. This emphasizes once again its supplementary nature.

The person of the Holy Spirit By this we mean that the Holy Spirit is not to be regarded merely as an influence or energetic force emanating from God. He is as much a person as the Father and the Son within the Godhead. The Holy Spirit must never be referred to as 'It'. The basic evidence in Scripture is that both divine and personality attributes ascribed to the Father and to the Son are also given to the Holy Spirit. May I refer you to the section at the end of the book where you will find a full, but not exhaustive, list of biblical references. The personality of the Holy Spirit is essential if the activities attributed to him, alongside the Father and the Son, are to be upheld. If the foundation of any fabric is removed, the superstructure will collapse as a matter of course. Similarly ,if you take away the personality of the Spirit, very many passages in the Bible will need to be rewritten. For example, you cannot lie to or grieve the Holy Spirit if he is only an influence or energetic force (Acts 5:3, Eph.4:30). Such properties demand personality.

The whole tone of Scripture recognises the Spirit as a person. This is especially true in John's Gospel. When Jesus said 'He (the Father) will give you another Comforter' (14:16), the word he used for 'another' denotes another of the same kind -*allos*. He might have used the word *heteros*, meaning another of a different kind; but he did not, and that is significant. It is equally impossible to read such passages as 14:26 and 16:13-14 and not have in mind a person, as opposed to an influence. Smeaton says of these verses (p.102), 'The use of the masculine demonstrative pronoun *(ekeinos)* forestalls the possibility of putting any other sense than a personal reference upon the words'. Consider a direct translation of 16:13-14 and notice the emphatic use of the personal pronoun. 'Howbeit, when he *(ekeinos)* the Spirit of Truth is come he will guide you into all the truth, for he will not speak from himself; but whatsoever he shall hear, that shall he speak, and he will show you things to come. He *(ekeinos)* shall glorify me'.

The Holy Spirit in the Life of Jesus There are no 'birth' narratives in John's Gospel. It is Luke who relates the work of the Holy Spirit to the Incarnation (Luke 1:35). This verse shows us that our Lord's humanity was not born of Adam's line and was therefore sinless, not being affected by the 'fall'. John's contribution to this is in 3:11-13, where Jesus speaks of his divine origin, and 13:3, where John adds his own comment, but no mention of the Spirit is made. That the Holy Spirit was constantly at work in Jesus throughout his earthly ministry is never in question. The Spirit was, in fact, given to him in abundant measure (3:34). The descent of the Holy Spirit in the form of a dove is mentioned in 1:32, but it is given greater emphasis in Matthew 3:16 and Luke 3:21, where the voice from heaven is recorded, 'This is my Son with whom I am well pleased'. John records the testimony of the Baptist, who notices something very significant - the dove 'remained on him'. This could well signify that all of our Lord's ministry was carried out by the continual presence of the Spirit, which was not the experience of God's children until after

Pentecost. John is singularly silent on the subject of the Spirit at work in Christ throughout his ministry. He seems to rely upon the testimony of the synoptics and the witness of the Baptist to establish this fact. It may interest readers to consider the following texts which have a bearing upon this; Matthew 4:1; Luke4:14; 17f. (Is a. 61:1-2); Matthew 12:28; Hebrews 9:14 and 1 Peter3:18.

The question is often asked, 'Why would Jesus, as the Son of God, need the Holy Spirit at all? We have to see the descent of the Spirit as the anointing of Christ for his three-fold ministry as Prophet, Priest and King. Those receiving these offices in the Old Testament were anointed with oil, symbolizing the Spirit of God equipping them for their separate tasks (e.g.Exodus 30:30, 1Sam.15:1,17). The dove, as the outward sign of the Spirit's descent upon Christ, is a witness to us, and a confirmation to the human Jesus, of his appointment by the Father to his mediatorial ministry.

The Baptism of the Holy Spirit. *1:34*.. For a full treatment of this subject I would refer readers to I Believe in the Holy Spirit (chap. 8, p.123-47), by Michael Green. It is way beyond the limits of a small book to deal with the subject here, but it should be mentioned that there are seven occasions in the New Testament where baptism with the Holy Spirit is mentioned. The four Gospels record the promise given by the Baptist that Jesus would baptize with the Holy Spirit (Matt.3:11; Mark 1:8; Luke3:16 and John1:33). In Acts 1:5, Jesus reminds the disciples of the Baptist's words and tells them that Pentecost would be the moment when that promise was fulfilled. In Acts 11:16, Peter is retelling the events that took place in the house of Cornelius,and he recounts how the Gentiles had a similar experience as did the Jews on the day of Pentecost. This he identifies with the baptism of the Holy Spirit. Michael Green points out that John baptized with water as a mark of repentance, but Jesus baptized with the Holy Spirit to bring men into the blessings of the New Covenant, which became possible on the Day of Pentecost What are we saying? Simply that the new birth is our individual Pentecost. The final reference teaches exactly the same thing, as one would expect, that 'By one Spirit we were all baptized into one body...and all made to drink of one Spirit' (1Cor. 12:13). We need to remember that this verse was written against the background of a church which was troubled by those who were making claims to what they believed to be a special baptism of the Spirit, which enabled them to exercise all kinds of spiritual ministries. No, says Paul: all who are Christians have been baptized by the Spirit. It is this which initiates them into the New Covenant of grace. One of the most important facts to notice is that, following Pentecost, we do not read of anyone being baptized with the Holy Spirit. It was the once-for-all event anticipated in the Gospels, realised in Acts2, and now available for all who believe. It is unbiblical for anyone to have a spiritual experience, subsequent to conversion, and refer to it as the baptism of the Holy Spirit. That many do have such experiences is without question, but it is not the baptism of the Spirit. If I was asked, 'What then is this kind of experience which so many in these days of renewal are enjoying?', I would have to suggest that it could well be due to a deeper surrender of oneself to Christ, which would open up fresh areas of one's life in which the Spirit would have a new freedom to work. We must always remember that it is one thing for us to have all of Christ: it is another for him to have all of us. Michael Green offers one further thought which should be mentioned: 'Christians are never told to wait or pray for the baptism of the Holy Spirit. The reason, of course, is that, being Christians, they have already been thus baptized.

Born of the Spirit *(3:5-8).*

The phrase comes three times in chapter 3, and nowhere else in the Gospel. It clearly means the same as being born 'again' or 'from above', but is intended to provide us with more detail. The association of the Spirit with water would indicate water in baptism, which is the outward and visible sign of the invisible cleansing and renewing work of the Spirit. We must be careful to note that the suggestion is not that baptism confers the Spirit, but that the water is significant of the Spirit's activity in the new birth experience. We saw, when considering the Prologue, that there is no way a person can bring about his own spiritual birth. Jesus is saying that it is the Holy Spirit who is the means whereby this new life from God is received.

The Spirit in worship (4:19-24).

Jesus had been speaking with the Samaritan woman at the well of Sychar. The place is not quite so accessible today as it was some twenty years ago. Then, most pilgrims to the Holy Land were taken to what is a fairly authentic holy place. The well there is truly 'deep'(v.11). The little town nestles close by Mount Gerizim, the holy mountain of the Samaritans. When the woman said to Jesus, 'Our fathers worshipped in this mountain' (v.20), there is little doubt she had Gerizim in mind. Some have suggested that, in the conversation with Jesus, the sudden transition from her marriage problem to worship was due to her embarrassment. But she was more than embarrassed, she was puzzled. The Samaritans did not accept the authority of the prophets, and yet here was this man exposing her inner life. How could she possibly deny his validity? She seems to have been drawn into the conversation which followed. Was this an occasion of Chapter 6:44? Hendriksen sees the Holy Spirit already at work in her heart (p.166).

The conversation Jesus had with this Samaritan woman is fascinating. The questions it raises are numerous. If conviction of sin was beginning to work in her, it is possible that she was seeking to know the authority with which this prophet spoke. Which religion is right - yours or mine? The Temple at Jerusalem was central to Jewish worship because God had said, 'There I will meet with you'. So which is it to be - Mount Zion or Mount

Gerizim? If, in verse 21, Jesus had the destruction of Jerusalem in mind, neither mountain was of any consequence. 'You Samaritans' (v.22, the word is plural) worship in ignorance. The true knowledge of God has been given to Israel that through them the message of salvation might come to the world. When that salvation is revealed, Zion or Gerizim will be of little significance. The Father will look for worship according to the truth (his revelation) which is offered from within by the inspiration of the Spirit.

The whole concept of earthing worship is dismissed in verse 24. God is Spirit. God is not corporial in the human sense. True worship is not to be limited to material things. God is not tied to buildings, localities and liturgies. This does not mean that church buildings, customs and ceremony have no place in worship. On the contrary, experience tells us that we need such things, but they are not the preordained channels through which true worship can only be offered.

John is not slow to record how Jesus revealed his true Messianic authority toward the end of the conversation. The phrase 'I am the one' in this verse 26 is never included in the well known list of the seven 'I am' phrases but it is, nevertheless, as emphatic as any.

Receiving the Spirit *(7:37-9)* This question has been fully aired in Chapter 2 (The Prologue). There are so many different ways in which John, in his Gospel, speaks of a person receiving God into his life. Born again, or from above, having eternal life, receiving Christ, and here, receiving the Spirit, are all variants of this one great truth. One of the most powerful sections in the Gospel on this theme is in chapter 14:15-24, where we see not only the Son and the Spirit, but the Father also, taking up their residence within the life of a believer. Just think of it; the Trinity of the Godhead within each of his children. A single human life - my life - becomes the crucible of the Godhead. When this thought first came home to me I shook in wonderment. The Bible does not speak of any phenomenal experience which necessarily accompanies the event. It is one of those great theological facts that we simply believe and know what has come to pass on the basis that God said so. Here we are, back into chapter 20:31. Look at 11:25 again. Do you believe this?

The Work of the Holy Spirit. First, let us consider his name *'parakletos'*. Literally, it seems to mean 'called to the side of', with 'giving assistance' in mind. In Greek it is used of a legal advisor or an advocate. Hence you will find the word translated 'counsellor' in many New Testament translations. The word 'comforter' is not the best, and can easily convey the wrong meaning by suggesting that his work is primarily one of soothing. That is far from the truth. As always, the clearest meaning of any word is seen in the way in which it is used. So what does the 'paraclete' do? Let us confine our studies to the words of Jesus in the Upper Room.

i) He witnesses to Christ, *15:26*. This is truly his primary work. Wherever the Spirit is at work, there Christ will be glorified. He will see to it that in all things Christ is pre-eminent. I say it reverently, and I hope the reader will not misunderstand, but some Christians have so exalted the Spirit that the image of Christ has become blurred. He has been pushed into the background. If this is the case, I would seriously question whether it is the activity of the Spirit at all, because his great joy is to glorify Christ (16:14). Paul reminds us that Christ is the Head and the Beginning of the Body, the first fruits of those who rise from the dead, 'that in everything He might have the pre-eminence' (Col.1:18).

ii) He teaches and brings to light the mysteries of Christ*(14:26, 16:13-14)*. A good commentary on these verses is to be found in 2:22 and 12:16. Paul takes up the question of seeking to understand the deep things of God in 1Corinthians 2:10-16. He shows that the natural man is unable to discern the mysteries of God. Only the Spirit of God can know these things. The

Corinthian passage might be a good one to study in seeking to appreciate the truth of this. Barrett writes (p.408), 'The teaching of the Spirit is not merely inspiration in the ordinary sense: it is the teaching of God'.

iii) He exposes the sin of the world, the righteousness of Christ, and the judgement which is inevitable when these two meet *(16:8-11)*. The meaning of the word in the original, often translated 'convict' or 'convince', is 'to expose'. In verse 8 we are told what the Holy Spirit does. Verses 10 and 11 explain how he does it. Consider the question of sin. We have just seen that it is the Spirit who reveals the truth about Jesus. Not to believe in Him (Jesus) as the Christ, the Son of God, the Saviour of the world, exposes the unbeliever as still in his sin, because he does not recognize who Jesus is, and why he came. The world is condemned in sin because it does not believe in Jesus.

Consider the question of righteousness. Jesus is at the right hand of the Father because of his sinlessness. If you like, he alone could lay claim to a place in the heavenly kingdom because there was no sin in his life which would exclude him. The world may be exposed as sinful, but Jesus is exposed to the world as righteous because he has risen and ascended to his father on high. It is the Spirit who enables a believer both to see and accept this.

Consider the question of judgement. The death of Jesus involved the downfall of Satan (the ruler of this world). Satan may survive for a time, but his downfall at the final judgement is assured (Rev.20:10). It is the Spirit who alone convinces men of this fact of judgement.

We do well to note the words of Jesus about the Spirit in verse 13; 'When the Spirit of truth comes, he will guide you into all truth'.

iv) He will reveal things to come *(v13b)*. It is a mistake to ascribe futuristic utterances to these words. Jesus is not saying that the Holy Spirit will tell you what is going to happen in the future. In the original, the words mean 'the things that are coming', that is the imminent things: Christ's death, resurrection and ascension. After Pentecost, the apostles understood the meaning of these words and under the Spirit's authority became the interpreters of these events to the church.

Of course, there is much more to the ministry of the Spirit than has been dealt with in this chapter. But then we have just been sharing together some of the issues mentioned in the Fourth Gospel. If we could sum up his ministry, we might say that it is primarily to lead people into faith, and in doing so to glorify Christ. Has he yet been able to reveal to you that Jesus is the Christ, the Son of God, the Saviour of the world?

Questions for Discussion.

1) What difference does it make - knowing that the Holy Spirit is a person and not merely an energetic force from God?

2) Write in a sentence what you understand by the words 'He who baptizes with the Holy Spirit' (1:33). Share your findings with other members of the group.

3) What does it mean to worship in spirit and in truth? How would you distinguish between a congregation which, in your opinion, did, and a congregation which did not?

4) Which particular ministry of the Spirit makes its strongest appeal to you at this moment, and why do you think this is so?

CHAPTER 15

OUR LORD'S HIGH PRIESTLY PRAYER, *(17:1-26)*

It has often been said that the prayer our Lord taught the disciples to pray should be referred to as the Disciples' Prayer rather than the Lord's Prayer, because the address of the Son to the Father in chapter 17 is much more worthy of the title. It truly is the Lord's Prayer. It is the Son's longest address to the Father and is a wonderful example of simplicity when it comes to natural and unconventional conversation. As you would expect, however, it is also full of profound theology. It reminds me of the way my own father sometimes used to say to me at the end of a day, 'Well, and what have you been doing with yourself all day?'. I would then recount my doings in detail, especially if they included a task he had specifically asked me to do. Notice how Jesus reports his doings to the Father: 'I glorified thee on earth, having accomplished the work thou gavest me to do' (v.4). The Father was glorified in the doing of his will. God is always glorified when his will is carried out, even by the least of his children.

Chapter outline. The first sentence, 'When Jesus had spoken these words' (v.1), confirms that the prayer was offered in the presence of those who had shared in the Upper Room events. Verses 1 to 5 are concerned with the commission Jesus received from his Father. In verses 6 to 19, Jesus addresses the Father on behalf of his disciples. And from verse 20 to the end of the chapter, he has the world-wide church in mind.

Jesus reflects on the purpose of His coming *(v.1-3)*
The supreme moment of Christ's earthly ministry, his crucifixion, was upon him, and his prayer is that through it both he and his Father will be glorified, that is, achieve their desired end. The end is that all who come to know the Father, and Jesus Chris

whom he sent, shall receive eternal life as a gift from the Son. Verse 5 introduces the hope of the resurrection and the ascension. Because in his life Jesus had glorified the Father by his total obedience and was therefore sinless, he was worthy to inherit the kingdom in his own right. John does not record the Gethsemane prayer but you could pour all of Gethsemane into the latter part of verse 1.

We need to understand John's use of the word 'knowledge', otherwise verse 3 becomes a problem. What does Jesus mean by knowing God and Jesus Christ? Anyone wishing to engage in a full discussion on the subject of 'knowledge' should consult the second part of The Bible and the Greeks by C.H.Dodd, but for most of us involved in these studies a simple explanation may suffice. Nowhere does John use the word 'knowledge' in the same way as the Gnostics (referred to in the introduction), which generally involved a knowledge of the universe and mythical systems by which a person may climb to God. This was probably intentional on John's part. By doing so he not only disassociates the Christian Gospel from a common heresy but replaces it with a different concept of knowledge. With John it is a knowledge brought about by being united with God and experiencing him by virtue of the new birth. Knowing God in this personal and intimate fashion in no way contradicts 20:21, where, as we have seen, the new birth is brought about by 'believing'. Barrett says, 'Knowing and believing are not set over against one another but correlated' (Commentary on John p.420). Notice too, you cannot separate knowledge of the Father from knowledge of the Son(see also 14:7-10).

I have manifested thy Name *(v.6a)* The disciples must have felt very much drawn into the prayer as from this verse, because it relates particularly to them. He made known to them the true character and nature of the Father, and he did this through the revelation of himself (14:9).

I have given them the words you gave me *(v.8)* This word the disciples had believed and received. They were to be the interpreters of the truth to the world, and there was nothing they needed to know that had not been passed on to them. In receiving the word they had received the Life, the *Logos*, the Living Word.

I have kept them...guarded them *(v.12)* This prayer, that they may continue to be sustained and enabled for the task before them, must have been tremendously reassuring to the disciples. One very strong emphasis is that they may be kept 'holy' - untouched by the evil that is in the world, which comes from Satan himself, who is the source of all evil (v.15). The word's sanctify' in verse 17 is important to understand. It comes from the latin *sanctus*, which means 'separated unto', as does *hagios,* which is its Greek equivalent. They are in the world physically, but they must be separated unto the Word of Truth, just as Jesus was separated (same word) unto the task that was given to him. In no less a way, we also are meant to be 'separated unto' God, both in the quality of our lives and in the commission that has been given to us, whatever that may be. Some people have been a little disenchanted by certain extreme holiness movements. This is usually the case when rigid guidelines are laid down as to what you can and what you cannot do in the sanctifying process. The Bible is very clear on the question of how a disciple may become more like Christ. It is by submitting oneself to the revealed truth which is in God's Word (v.17). What we are talking about is 'living by the Book': that is by the grace of God bringing us under the authority of his Word. I say 'by the grace of God' because, as you will see from verse 17, sanctification is God's work which takes place in the willing soul. The believer reads the Word prayerfully and obediently, and God reveals the inner meaning and inspires the right response in obedience

I have sent them into the world *(v.18)* The apostles were the first agents sent into the world to preach the Gospel, but they were not the last. And so those who were present with Christ were left in no doubt as to their commission. They were to represent the continued presence of Christ in the world and exercise their unique ministry of apostleship which they alone could fulfil

The unity of the Body *(v.20-23)* From verse 20 Jesus turns his attention to the world-wide church, the universal body of Christ which spans generations. Those who accept the apostolic preaching are truly one, and share in this organic unity simply because they have received in common the life of God in Christ. It is this that makes them one It has nothing whatever to do with denominations. Perhaps it is as well that any decision as to who is, and who is not, within the body of Christ does not rest with individuals, or local churches for that matter,although we do know there are some who mistakenly claim this authority. Often it is because there is a misunderstanding as to what is meant by unity and oneness. If you mean a unity that is brought about by man-made institutions, then you are at cross purposes with what the Gospel is saying here. The key phrase is verse 23, 'I in them', and, as we have seen, this is brought about by believing. It is the only organic unity that can be identified in the New Testament. The pattern of this oneness is the Trinity itself, from which the body derives its life and strength. Through this perfect oneness the world would come to know that the love of God is in them.

A future hope *(24)* Some find it difficult to understand why Jesus would pray for his followers as he did, because he knew what their inheritance was. He also prayed in full accord with the Father's will and he knew what that was too (e.g.4:34; 5:30;6:38-9). So why does he pray this prayer? It may have something to do with 13:33-6, when the disciples seem to have been very discouraged. He now speaks of an occasion when they will be able to follow him, and so he lifts their spirits with this sure and certain hope that in the end the children of God will be with him in the eternal future, and there they will behold his true glory. But the end is not yet. There is still the earthly commission to come, which will launch them into the world with a Gospel to proclaim (vv.25-6). During this time they will be sustained by his indwelling, and because of this will manifest his love, which is to be the hall-mark of the church's witness in the world.

Questions for Discussion.

1) In every prayer Jesus prayed which is recorded in the Gospels, he prays to the Father (e.g. 17:1). Is this an unbending pattern for our praying, or can we also pray to the Son and to the Holy Spirit? There are many instances in our great liturgies where prayers are offered to all three members of the Trinity seperately, and to the Trinity itself. A simple formula for prayer has been offered, namely, 'We should pray to the Father through the Son in the power of the Holy Spirit'. Is this sacrosanct, or are there other legitimate ways in which we may approach God in prayer?

2) Jesus speaks of his Joy (v.1) 3 and his love (v.2) 6 being in his disciples. How might these two great graces manifest themselves in his disciples today?

3) What would you say was the meaning of the words 'I am glorified in them'? (v.10). Remember, in this part of the prayer the 'them' refers to the disciples who were with him in the Upper Room.

4) Consider the phrase 'that they may become perfectly one' (or, 'attain perfect unity') (v.23). What is meant by perfect unity? Does this mean absolute uniformity?

CHAPTER 16

THE PASSION IN JOHN

A friend of mine once had a dream that he was standing by the Cross when Jesus was crucified. 'What was your reaction?' I asked him. 'I was horrified', he said, 'and the worst part was that I woke up screaming "Crucify Him!", "Crucify Him!"' I did not quite know what to say to him but, after a pause, he looked at me straight in the eye and added 'I learned one thing, though; there are no spectators of Calvary; we are all participants'. And, of course, he was theologically right. We are all involved in the death of Christ because it was the sin of each one of us that made his sacrifice necessary in the work of salvation. Disclaiming involvement, or having a total disregard for what happened on that momentous day, no more absolves me than did the bowl of water absolve Pilate of the part he played in Christ's death (Matt.27:24).

The Cross of Christ is the focal point of all four Gospels, each evangelist making his own distinctive contribution to both the record and the meaning. The theme is so central to the Christian message that I am sure I will be forgiven if I venture a little further than the fourth Gospel by considering the records of all four evangelists - if only to show, in brief, how each Gospel in its turn complements the others. I will, of course, be giving a little more attention to what John has to say.

St Matthew looks at the Cross. His overwhelming contribution is that he sees the Cross as the fulfilment of Old Testament prophecy. In this he is not unique, as all the evangelists insist that the crucifixion was a fulfilment of Scripture (Mark14:49; Luke 24:44; John 19:24,36), but none so consistently as Matthew. The main reason for this is because his Gospel was

113

written for Jewish readers and he constantly looks to the Old Testament for his authority. He it is who quotes Jesus assaying, 'I am come to fulfil the law and the prophets' (Matt.5:17; 8:16-17; 12:17-21,40). When we come to the Passion narratives, it is almost as though Matthew is recounting the events with the Old Testament in his hand. Maybe he was. 'It is all here', he would say; 'see for yourselves. Take the Scriptures and consider how every detail of what was foretold concerning the Messiah has been fulfilled in Jesus of Nazareth'. The triumphal entry (21:5,9,13,16,42) the garden of Gethsemane (26:54-6), the thirty pieces of silver (27:9), and the crucifixion itself (27:30,35,60), all come in for special mention.

St Mark looks at the Cross. The key verse in this the earliest Gospel is 10:45, 'The Son of Man came not to be ministered unto but to minister and give his life a ransom for many'.   In chapters 1 to 10 Jesus is portrayed as the servant of men. In chapters 11 to 16 it is his life that is paid for their ransom. St Mark is the interpreter of Peter, and so we see the Cross as Peter saw it. An interesting observation is that, at first, Peter objected violently to any suggestion that Jesus should suffer at the hands of men (Mark 8:31-3). As you read and re-read the Gospel, however, it seems as though every effort is made to put right his error.   No less than one third of the book is devoted to the Passion and the emphasis is that the Cross is an inevitable fulfilling of the divine plan. From 1:15, 'the time has come', God's purposes gradually and inevitably unfold. If the reader would like to see this theme through, the following texts may be helpful: 8:31, 9:31, 10:33-4,45. See also 14:8, the anointing; 14:21, the Son of Man must tread the path of Calvary; 14:24, anticipating the shed blood; 14:36 Gethsemane ('Your will be done'); and 15:31, before the chief priests.

St Luke looks at the Cross. Matthew, a Jew writing to Jews, sees the Cross as the fulfillment of the Old Testament. Peter through Mark, portrays the Cross as the fulfilment of the divine will. Luke writes as a Gentile for Gentile readers. He was a doctor (of medicine), a literary scholar (his Greek is far and away the best of all the Gospels) who became a companion of St Paul. Luke emphasizes the intense suffering of the Cross: not only the physical, but also the mental suffering through which Jesus passed. One might expect this from a doctor. If St Mark's Gospel is dramatic, St Luke's is certainly emotional and intensely human. It is the Gospel with which people most easily identify.

There is a great deal in Luke which is also in Matthew and Mark. If you consider the passages which are peculiar to Luke and those which, if not altogether peculiar nevertheless give some special emphasis, you will notice several things:

He stresses the determination of Christ to suffer. In 9:31, notice the word 'accomplish', which is a striking way of seeing the Cross as an 'achievement'. Again, in 9:51-3 'He set his face'. Some have seen the same determination in 22:37, 'have its fulfilment' or 'have its end purpose'. In Luke, intention to suffer intensifies the suffering.

He stresses the activity of the enemy in Christ's suffering, not only human foes but also satanic. In this way the greater intensity of the battle is highlighted (22:3): 'Then entered Satan into Judas' (see also 22:53, 'this is your hour and the power of darkness'). In 23:4-12, Luke records our Lord before Herod and mentions the Jewish King's dicey friendship with Pilate which emerged. He sees the enemy gathering together against Jesus.

He stresses the many emotions of Christ during the trial and crucifixion. In Luke 22:50-1 Luke alone records the actual healing. In 22:60-1, it is Luke who adds the words 'the Lord turned and looked upon Peter'. The doctor notices the inner psychological implications and is instinctively aware of the intense feeling Jesus experienced at that moment. It is a surprise to many to learn that only Luke records the words of Jesus on the Cross, 'Father, forgive them, for they know not what they do' (22:34), and also 'Today shalt thou be with me in paradise' (23:43), both of which stress the deep compassion of our Lord.

He stresses the incomprehensible mental and spiritual suffering of Jesus. He alone notices the great drops of sweat that fell as blood to the ground. He alone is aware of the supernatural support that came to him during those moments of incomparable agony (2:43-4).

He stresses the need for the disciples to have a death-resurrection experience *(9:22-3)*. Notice the words 'all' and 'daily' in verse 23. A well loved curate of mine, who is now with Christ, once said to me of a very proud and offensive parishioner, 'that man needs to go into a corner and die to himself'. Luke would have agreed.

St John looks at the Cross There are nine chapters in the Gospel which are devoted specifically to the events surrounding the Passion and Resurrection of Christ. The Cross as a subject,however, is in evidence throughout the Gospel. It is not referred to in the Prologue because its purpose is to introduce the person of Christ and not illucidate upon his ministry. Even before his ministry begins, however, John the Baptist introduces him as 'the Lamb of God' (1:29,36), where he is said to 'take away the sin of the world'. The first of his statements that his 'hour (time) had not come' appears as early as 2:4. Some have suggested that Jesus meant the moment for him to begin his earthly ministry had not yet arrived. But we cannot sustain such weak comments, if only because he often uses the phrase after he had begun his public work. Also, it has to be seen in the light of his words when the Cross was almost upon him 'the hour has come' (e.g. 12:23, 27; 13:1; 16:32; 17:1). There are many other occasions when his Passion was uppermost in his mind. Consider, for instance, 2:18-21; 3:14; 8:28;12:32-4; and also some of the 'I am' passages (6:51, 10:11-14,11:25). Further passages, such as 3:16-17; 11:50 all allude to his passion, and there are many more. From chapter 13 the references are legion and obvious. What then might we conclude is John's special contribution to our understanding of the Passion of Christ?

Jesus on the Cross is the Lamb of God slain as a sacrifice for the sin of the world. At this point the student would do well to read Exodus 12:1-14, the Lord's Passover. It helps us to see the relevance of 1:29. I once heard a minister state publicly that he never preached from the Old Testament because it was out of date. During question time he was asked to explain John 1:29 without reference to the Old Testament. Of course he could not and I do not think I have ever seen anyone more embarrassed. You may like to consider 1John 1:7; Revelation1:5, 5:9, 7:14, to note how John homes in on this emphasis throughout his writings.

Jesus on the Cross is the moment of his supreme glory *(John13:31-2).* This is very closely linked with Jesus as the Lamb of God, because the Lamb slain is the glory of heaven (Rev.5:8-9,12; 7:10; 21:22-3; 22:3). It is interesting to observe Paul re-echoing John here (Gal.6:14).

Jesus on the Cross is the supreme act of God's love *(John3:16; 13:1; 1John 4:10; Rev.1:5).* Have you ever realized that, apart from Mark 10:21, 'Jesus beholding him, loved him', John provides the only references in the Gospels where Jesus is spoken of as loving someone?

As with our study on the Holy Spirit, our approach to the Passion has been rather thematic. This is inevitable because the subject goes right through the Gospel. A good conclusion to this kind of approach is to read through the Gospel, noting every verse which relates to the theme in question. Not only is it one of the best ways to become familiar with the Bible but you will certainly come across many passages which have purposely not been mentioned above.

Questions for Discussion.

1) Can your group give a comprehensive view of the Cross by bringing together the particular contribution of each of the evangelists?

2) What passages have you come across in the Gospel which might be added to those suggested as relating to the Passion?

3) How would you describe the significance of Jesus being called 'the Lamb of God', and how does it relate to faith and forgiveness?

4) What difference can a clear understanding of the suffering of Christ make to one's daily life?

5) What is evangelism and how can we be involved in it?

CHAPTER 17

A GALILEAN RESURRECTION APPEARANCE

An Appendix to the Gospel (ch.21)

Most of the resurrection appearances were in and around Jerusalem, but in John 21 we have a Galilean appearance when our Lord met with some of his disciples by the Sea of Galilee. It would seem that the occasion was prompted by the events of Mark 16:1-8. Certainly Peter, who was especially mentioned in Mark 16:7, is the central figure in the drama of John 21.

Having come to the penultimate chapter in this study book, it seems appropriate that we conclude with two chapters of a very personal and practical nature. There is no doubt that John's intention in writing his Gospel was that the reader should come to believe on the Lord Jesus Christ and be saved from the consequences of his sin and receive new life from above. But what then? Is he to continue living in the security of his own salvation without any thought for the salvation of others? Not a bit of it, and in these final chapters we shall be looking at Christ's commission to his converts. First (in ch.21) 'Feed my Sheep', and secondly (in ch.20) 'As my Father has sent me so I send you'. I hope the reason for reversing the chapter order will become clear as we proceed.

There were seven who went fishing (v.2). They were impetuous Peter, doubting Thomas, guileless Nathaniel, unpredictable James and John (called Sons of Thunder by Jesus, John being the beloved disciple). With them were two others. They are unlikely to have been apostles, otherwise their names would almost certainly have been mentioned. They were less prominent disciples, possibly less gifted, but they were there, unknown, yet important to God. It leaves the door wide open for anyone to feel they might well have been in the party. And a very fruitless night they had (v.3). It was at the side of this very lake that Jesus had originally called his first disciples with those memorable words 'Come, follow me, and I will make you to become fishers of men' (Matt 4:19). We may well ask, Did Jesus arrange to meet these men in Galilee because he wanted to remind them of his original calling? Certainly there are remarkable links. Not only does he enable them to make a fine catch, and in so doing reveal some of the principles which lie behind effective ministry, but he also has a conversation with Peter about 'following him'. What memories this must have bought of the former occasion when the call to follow was made, with the promise that if they followed him he would make them not fishers of fish but of men. What might the disciples have deduced from all this? Were they living out a parable? We observe four things of considerable interest:

He manifested his presences in a time of extreme *loneliness (v.4,7)* Peter seems to have expressed the despair of the disciples in verse 3. They were a group of dispirited men in the midst of hostility, cynicism and indifference - not unlike the world in which the twentieth century disciple has to live. If any disciple has a desire to make Christ known, he too will feel the cold draught of loneliness. Not a little comfort can be drawn from remembering that Jesus knew all about such pressures. He was tempted in all points as we are, and yet was not overcome by the severe testing through which he passed (Heb.4:15-16). So we find him drawing near to his disciples, encouraging them in their loneliness and despair. Do we sometimes feel dispirited? He is never far away.

He manifested His power in the time of *weakness (v.6)* Unlike drama on television, we do not hear most of the conversation which passed between these rugged fishermen while they were toiling through the night. It does not demand great imagination, however, to hear one of them refer to the events of Luke 5:4-11 and remark that it was a pity the Lord was not there to help out. They might even have added, 'I wonder what he meant about "catching men"?' (Luke 5:10). There must have been something very compelling and reassuring about the man on the shore who enquired after their welfare and spoke so authoritatively (vv.5-6). Now, who caught the fish? Factually, it was the disciples. Truly, it was the Lord, and it was this factor which John immediately recognised and recorded (v.7a). Had the disciples the eyes to see it, they may well have recognized that just as his ability came to the rescue of their weakness and failure in catching fish, so it would be in winning men for Christ. It is a principle which is true for every area of Christian experience, whether it is in personal growth or in ministry. We need to recognize our need of him in all things. Once we think we can achieve anything in our own strength, we lay ourselves open to failure. As St Paul said, 'When I am weak, then I am strong' (2 Cor.12:10). So we give the credit to him. God can do anything with a person who is willing to give all the glory to him.

He manifested his provision in a *time of need (v.9)* It would be foolish to assume that we can deduce from this verse that Jesus will overload his children with goodies. I mention this because there is a school of thought which says that one of the blessings of being a Christian is that one will prosper in every area of life, including earthly possessions. This is a theory which is not proven in Scripture, nor in the experience of the church throughout the ages. These men were tired and hungry and Jesus provided for their basic needs (see Phil.4:19). The emphasis here is more in the realm of God's concern for the simple, basic necessities of life. What a remarkable thing it is. Our Lord had just been crucified. He had passed through the descent into hell and the resurrection experience. His ascension was almost upon him and his mind must have been full of the great reunion with his Father that was about to take place. He was shortly to initiate the great event of Pentecost by sending the Holy Spirit to usher in the new dispensation. Yet he made the time to prepare a simple meal for these tired and hungry men. The lesson has to be that God is as much concerned about the little as well as the big things in my life. Basic Christian teaching is that God will supply all that is needed for his children to fulfill his purpose in their lives.

He manifested his purpose in a time of *self-abasement* (v.15-22) . We have already noticed that Jesus particularly wanted to speak with Peter. As the apostle gazed into the burning brazier, it seems more than likely that his mind was upon an earlier occasion when he had stood warming his hands at another fireside (18:18,25-7). By verse 12 the disciples were well aware that the stranger on the shore was Jesus and it was no surprise to Peter to be approached by the Lord. Peter had a conscience that was troubling him and there was a matter concerning his relationship with Jesus that needed attention. Jesus, knowing this, engages Peter in conversation and there is a hint in verse 20 that they walked together beside the lake.

I have often referred to verses 15-22 as the 'Collapse of Self Confidence' and, at the risk of going over what to some readers may be old ground, we should take a look at the different words used in the narrative in the original language but translated by the same word 'love' in most of our Bible versions. It brings out the gentle yet positive way in which Jesus helped Peter to overcome his biggest fault, that of self-confidence. We should always have 12:36-8 in mind when considering 21.15-19.

'Agapao' and *'Phileo'*. The first word is the stronger of the two and is used to describe the love which God has for his children (14:21), and the love which he asks from them (14:23). It is also the word that is used when references are made of the love that exists within the Godhead. That, of course, is putting it very simply, but nevertheless it is relevant. A good commentary on this thought would be 1John 4:7-12. The second word literally means 'to be a friend of' and can easily be seen to mean something quite different. When Jesus speaks to Peter (v.15) he uses

the stronger word but, in his reply, Peter, remembering how he had denied his Lord, feels he cannot rise to the occasion and says 'Yes, Lord, you know I am your friend'. In spite of this (or was it because of it?), Jesus says to him, 'Feed my lambs'. In verse 16 the same two words are used by both Jesus and Peter except that Jesus tells him not to 'feed' the lambs but to 'shepherd' (different word) 'the little sheep' (also a different word). On the third occasion, however, Jesus comes down to Peter's level (v.17) and says, 'Are you really a friend to me?'. No wonder Peter was grieved. His reply reveals how aware he was that Jesus looks deep into the hearts of men: 'Lord, you know I am, you know everything, you know precisely the state of my heart'. Jesus said to him, 'Feed my little sheep'. Verse 19a is an editorial comment by John written in the light of Peter's subsequent martyrdom.

The passage actually recognizes that with all of us there is a human limit to the quality of the love we can offer our Lord. But what we can, we must offer; and what we offer, God accepts. This is born out by the fact that Jesus then goes on to unfold, in a few words, the sacrificial way in which Peter would both live and die for the one who truly became his Lord. He then commissions Peter to follow him, which Peter does all the days of his earthly pilgrimage, for that is what it was. Verses 20-3 remind us that our first concern must always be to fulfill our own calling rather than be unduly troubled about the calling of others.

Questions for Discussion.

1) Bearing in mind the events of Matthew 4 and Luke 5, are we justified in drawing out such spiritual truths as have been mentioned above? What would you say were the limits to such spiritualizing, and did Jesus ever do this with the Old Testament? (This is a question aimed at assisting us in our approach to understanding the Bible.)

2) In what ways do you think God assists us in our failures and weaknesses? Can you share any such experiences with other members of the group?

3) Discuss Philippians 4:19. Do you accept that God calls some to wealth and others to poverty in the cause of reaching all sorts and conditions of people?

CHAPTER 18

GREATER LOVE HATH NO MAN THAN THIS *(15:13)*

I make no apologies if this final chapter comes over more like a sermon than an introduction to a group Bible study. My principal at theological college used to say, 'If, when you are preaching, your handling of God's Word does not leave the congregation with a challenge to face and a decision to make, you may well have failed'. The same could quite easily be said of a book of this nature, and I hope many decisions have already been made during the studies. There is, however, one issue I rate above every other and I want to think about it with you in this final chapter.

The main purpose of the Gospel is clearly stated in 20:31, and this we have looked at many times. There is also an overriding theme which you may well have noticed: it is 'Love'. There is so much about love in the Gospel. Love is the essence of the Trinity (3:35; 15:9-11). It is because God loves the world that he sent his only Son (3:16). It is not stoic obedience that God wants from his children. It is love from which obedience flows, because love is the fulfilling of the law. It was to be the spirit which dominated the New Testament people of God (13:31:4). It is in loving that God is glorified (15:8). Love is the criterion by which the experience of God's indwelling may be known (14:23), and it is that by which all men would be able to discern the true disciples of Jesus (13:35). The Gospel closes with Jesus confronting Peter on the question of love (ch.21) and John, the beloved disciple, was its author.

There are very few people who do not accept that love is the greatest of all virtues. Certainly the Christian faith teaches this (see 1 Cor.13). We are also told that the first fruit of the Spirit is love (Gal.5:22). We can go further than this and say that there is no greater love than the love of God in Christ. If we could measure love, it would be on the basis of the way it expresses itself. So, when God wanted to commend his love toward us, he sent his Son (John 3:16a; Rom.5:8). We can even take it a stage further and say that God never expressed his love more strongly than when Jesus died on the Cross (15:13). Bishop Lunt tells of an occasion when a railway worker, who had lost his son in a tragic accident, walked into his church in Stepney while he was preaching. The man stood half-way down the aisle and, pointing to a stained glass window portraying a Father-Neptune-type figure of God, blurted out, 'There he is, damn him, what does He care!'. There was another stained glass window on which was reproduced an artist's impression of Calvary. The bishop came down from the pulpit, went to the man who was overcome with grief and, turning him gently to the other window, put his arm about him and simply said 'that's how much he cares'. Of course, this great theological truth needed some explanation, and after the service the bishop was able to show him how this was so and the man took his first faltering steps into faith. Using John 3:16, I want to do the same, drawing several illustrations from the Gospel.

> 'For God so loved the world that he gave his one and
> only Son, that whoever believes in him shall not
> perish but have eternal life'.

The Persons it involves. 'God...the world'.

Why should God love us? More especially, why should God love me? As the psalmist said, 'what is man that God should be mindful of him?' (Psalm 8:4). Of course it astonishes us. Where would you find a love which fastened itself upon someone so far removed from the one who does the loving? Sometimes a person of royal blood marries a commoner, but this is not really a parallel. Royalty may bring prestige, wealth, honour and the glitter of the royal palace to the new relationship, but the commoner can bring even greater graces of intellect, beauty of character, and the like. In every case of human relationships the one either enriches or spoils the other. Not so with Christ and us, for he is infinitely above us in everything. For example: consider his moral excellencies. He is without sin (2Cor.5:21), while all our righteousness is likened to an unclean discarded rag (Is a. 64:6). With regard to knowledge, there is an immeasurable gulf between us. As the heavens are higher than the earth, so are his ways and thoughts compared to ours (Is a.55:8-9). As to everlastingness, he is 'from everlasting to everlasting' (Psalm 41:13), but from dust we came and to the dust we shall return (Job 34:15). The gulf that separates us is enormous. So we come back to the question, what is there about God that he should actually love me?

I was once leading a home Bible study group in North Africa and I posed this very question. It was some time before I got the answer for which I was looking, but when it came it was very beautifully and simply expressed: 'I think he loves me because he made me - an expression of his love'. There was a brief pause, then she added, 'and he saw that it was very good'. Exactly! We are, in fact, extensions of his person - rather like a craftsman who is delighted with his handiwork, only to perfection (see Gen.1:31). Sadly, the image was marred through disobedience. But a good father does not love his child any the less because he is sometimes disobedient. When my own children were rather naughty, as they were sometimes, I think I loved them even more because of their frailty.

The purity it reveals 'The world'.

No less than four times in two verses (1:16 and 17), John uses the phrase 'the world'. What John says about the world in his writings is important because it shows that God's love for us in no way depends upon our love for him. The world is God's fallen creation. Light came into the world and the world rejected the light because it is a sinful world and preferred its own darkness (1:9,

8:12). Such was his love for the world that he came to save it from judgement (4:42, 12:47), to take away the sin (1:29), and give it life - his life (3:16-17, 6:33). Satan may be its ruler (13:31) but he is its Saviour, and all who believe the truth will receive the life (14:22-3). When two people fall in love, one of the most exciting things is that they can both love each other with the same kind of love. The element in their relationship which makes for development and enrichment is that their love is equally reciprocal. But, as Paul puts it so clearly, 'God commended his love toward us while we were yet sinners' (Rom.5:8). It was, in fact, toward those who were unworthy to receive it, unwilling to respond to it, and unable to reciprocate it. The truth is that when God in Christ offered his love to the world, it was rejected (1:11). In other words,God sent his love into the world and it crucified him. God's love for us is pure love because even though we are sinful - that is, we can contribute little to enrich the relationship and are totally unworthy of His attention - his love for us is nevertheless perfect and unrestrained. It is entirely without self-gratification and totally for the benefit of those loved. This aspect of God's love is so beautifully reflected in the parable of the Prodigal Son. We read, 'While he (the prodigal) was a great way off, his father saw him, had compassion on him, and ran and embraced him and kissed him', Luke 15:20. Such is the purity of God's love for us.

The passion it displays 'He gave His only Son'

To do anything 'with passion' is to express oneself with fervour to the point of excess, in the sense of 'beyond what is normal'. When we refer to Christ's Passion we always have in mind his suffering on the Cross. Love never expressed itself more magnificently than this. We think of love showing itself in three ways and at three levels. By speech, when one person says to another, 'I love you'. By service, and here we add a new dimension, 'I will show you I love you'. Finally, by sacrifice,'I will show you how much I love you'. This is the declaration,the demonstration and the deprivation of love. And at every level the love of God in Christ excels all.

Consider the *declaration* of his love. 'I have loved you with an everlasting love' *(Jer.31:3)*. There never was a time when the love of God was not poured out toward his children. It is interesting to notice that this declaration was made at a time of Israel's disobedience. The most any of us can ever say is, 'I have loved you from the first moment I saw you', and how often have those words been taken with a pinch of salt! But God, with infinite ways of declaring his love, in his perfection could never exaggerate.

Consider the *demonstration* of his love. See him moving among the demented, the sick, the despised, the lost, the weak, the frightened, the lonely and so on. There was no one he would not touch, nowhere he would not go, no time at which he would not come, and nothing he was unwilling to do. Here we have Eternal Love expressing itself in the divine availability.

Consider the *deprivation* of his love. By this we mean the measure of his self sacrifice: 'Greater love has no man than this, that a man lay down his life for his friends' (15:13). It has often been pointed out that many have gallantly laid down their lives for others, and often in the cause of love. There is, however, a significant feature about Christ's death for us. It was 'while we were yet sinners', 'ungodly', 'enemies', that Christ died for us, (Rom.5:6-10). It was not man for man but God for man - the Creator for the created. There is also the significance of *'Eloi, Eloi, Lama Sabacthani'*, 'My God, My God, why hast thou forsaken Me?' (Mark 15:34). This does not mean that the Trinity was destroyed, but that the fellowship within it was momentarily crushed, and we can never know the awful agony Jesus endured when the Father turned his back upon him. The real pain of Calvary was not physical, but spiritual and within. On the Cross, God laid on his Son the iniquity of the world (Is a. 53:4-6), and being of 'purer eyes than to behold evil' (Hab.1:13), he turned away from the Cross, where every sin man ever committed was thrust upon Jesus. I am not saying that there is no deprivation in a sacrifice one person may make for another. What I am saying is that there never was self-deprivation like this, and never has the world witnessed such a magnificent expression of love as when Jesus died on the Cross. When he hung there, with his arms 'voluntarily' stretched out, he was, in fact, saying to the world in the clearest voice possible,'I love you!'.

The peace it brings 'whoever believes...shall not perish'.

The Good News (the Gospel) is that Jesus has taken upon himself the guilt of our sin and endured the consequences of it - separation from God - that 'whoever believes' might be reconciled to God. This is what Paul means when he says in Romans 5:10; 'While we were enemies, we were reconciled to God by the death of his Son'. When two people who have been estranged, are reconciled, it is because the cause of estrangement has been dealt with and there is forgiveness. On the Cross, Jesus removed the cause of estrangement, because he is the only one who could, and whoever accepts it is forgiven. A reconciled person is one who has made his peace with God (see Rom.5:1-11). You may think that a Roman cross, with a stricken body on it, is a strange way for God to show his love. Yet if you can see that the crucifixion was not simply an unjust execution but a love-offering for the sin of the world, then it takes on a whole new meaning, and verses like John 3:16 suddenly come to life. In previous chapters we have given much thought to believing and receiving. We have seen that, in John's Gospel, it means to accept Jesus as Son of God, Saviour and Lord and to submit oneself to the authority of his word. It is in this that we find forgiveness of sin and can be assured of his presence with us throughout eternity. If you have never faced such a challenge before, are you ready to do so now?

When I was about seven years old, an aunt of mine, who was a well-known artist, was commissioned to paint the Coronation Coach. The painting was to appear in an encyclopedia, and as far as I know the original is still with the royal family. After several visits to the palace, the final touches to the work were done in her studio, which was situated on the top floor of our house. When it was finished, she invited my father to have a look at it. Unknown to them, I followed. After my father had offered some very complimentary remarks, they left the studio. I had a good look at the painting, hardly dry from the last brush strokes, and decided I could improve it. This I attempted to do, and unashamedly went down to auntie and told her what I had done. I leave the reader to imagine the rest. She rushed upstairs and spent days putting it right. After all, she was the only one who could. Of course, I got an awful wigging from my father who told me, when the disfigurements had been dealt with, to go to auntie and say how sorry I was, ask her to forgive me, and promise never to do such a thing again. This I did: 'Auntie, I'm very sorry for what I did'. What was that,dear?' she said. 'Your painting: will you please forgive me'. 'Oh that! I'd forgotten all about it'. She was a wonderful and understanding aunt. The analogy is obvious. Jesus is an even more wonderful, understanding and forgiving Saviour.

Now bring 3:16 and 20:31 together. Can you, with clearer understanding, make a personal commitment to Christ?

Questions for Discussion:

1) Discuss the truth or otherwise of the saying, 'God hates the sin but loves the sinner'.

2) Can anyone say categorically 'I have been born again; I am a child of God'?

3) If you have been helped to make a firm decision for Christ during these studies, do you think you could share it with the group?

SUPPLEMENT CONCERNING THE TRINITY

The purpose of this supplement is to show that titles and attributes given to God are given separately to the Father, the Son and the Holy Spirit. There is no method of biblical research which is better calculated to offer the emphatic claim that deity must be ascribed to all three persons of the Godhead, separately or together. For example: There is but one God who is eternal (Is a.41:4; 43:10; 44:6), and yet this divine attribute is ascribed to:

The Father,   Psalm 90:2; 93:2; 102:12

The Son,   Hebrews 13:8; Revelation 1:8, 17-18

The Holy Spirit, Hebrews 9:14

Each in his turn, therefore, must be understood as being God. Yet there is only one God (Deut. 6:4; Is a. 44:6-8). There must therefore be three persons in the one Godhead. John, in his Gospel, is most anxious to set Jesus forth as truly God. The following is given to show that this is, in fact, the clear teaching of the Bible. It is equally emphatic about the divine nature of the Holy Spirit. Consider the following:

Father —— Son ——— Holy Spirit

Titles Equally Given

GOD

John 17:3, John 1:1, Acts 5:3-4, Acts 20:28

LORD

Acts 4:24 ,1 Corinthians 8:6 , 2 Corinthians 3:16-7

The Holy Spirit is called the *Spirit of God,* 1 Corinthians 6:11 and the *Spirit of Christ,* Romans 8:9, Galations 4:6.

Perfections Equally Ascribed
ALMIGHTY
  2 Chronicles 20:26 Mt. 28:18, Zechariah 4:6
GOOD
  Mark 10:18, Acts 10:38, Nehemiah 9:20
TRUTH
  1 John 5:20, John 14:6, John 15:26
HOLY
  Revelation 4:8,Acts 3:14, 1 John 2:20
WISE
  Romans 11:33, Luke 2:40-52, Ephesians 1:17
ALL KNOWING
  Acts 15:18, John 21:17, 1 Corinthians 2:10

Operations Equally Credited
CREATOR
  Acts 14:15, John 1:3, Job 33:4
ONLY SAVIOUR
  Titus 3:4, Hebrews 7:25, Titus 3:5
FOREKNOWLEDGE
  Isaiah 42:9, John 18:4, 1 Peter 1:11, Revelation 22:6
FORETELLS
  Revelation 22:6, Luke 19:41-4, Luke 2:26
SOURCE OF LIFE
  Acts 17:25, John 1:4, Romans 8:2
LAWGIVER
  Exodus 20:1-19, John 13:34, Romans 8:2, John 15:12
RAISED CHRIST
  Acts 2:24, John 2:19, 1 Peter 3:18
NEW BIRTH
  John 1:13, 1 John 2:29, John 3:6
GIVES ETERNAL LIFE
  Romans 6:23, John 6:27, Galations 6:8

TEACHES SAINTS
Philippians 3:15, John 15:15, John 14:26,
GUIDES
Isaiah 48:17, 1 Peter 2:21, Romans 8:14
SANCTIFIES
1Thessalonians 5:23 Ephesians 5:26, Romans 15:16

Other ways of recognising the divine nature of the three Persons

CHRISTIANS ARE THE DWELLING PLACE OF
1 Corinthians 3:16 Ephesians 3:17, 1 Corinthians 6:19
CHRISTIANS ENJOY FELLOWSHIP WITH
John 17:21, 1 John 1:3, 2 Corinthians 13:14
SINNING IS TEMPTING THE
Deuteronomy 6:16, 1 Corinthians 10:9, Acts 5:9
THE WORLD HAS NOT KNOWN THE
1 Corinthians 1:21 John 1:10, John 14:27
BLESSINGS ARE GIVEN IN NAME OF TRINITY
Matthew 28:19, 2 Corinthians, 13:14, Numbers 6:24-6

References to the Triune nature of the Godhead are found in:Numbers 6:24-26; (Isaiah 6:3 & Revelation 4:8); Isaiah 43:14;Isaiah 48:16-17; Jeremiah 10:10; Matthew 3:16-17; Mark 1:10; Luke3:22; Acts 20:28; Romans 8:9; 15:18-19; 2 Corinthians 13:14;Galations 4:6; Ephesians 2:18; 2 Thessalonians 3:5; 1 Peter 1:2;1 John 5:4-7; Jude 20-21.

With some of the references given above, God's Triune nature is more implicit than explicit What is clear, however, is the overwhelming voice of Scripture giving support to the doctrine which lies at the heart of our great Christian creeds.

Comment on the Analysis

The purpose of the analysis which follows on the next two pages is to enable any reader, who may be unfamiliar with the Gospel's content, to find his way around the book more easily. It is, however, far better for the more advanced student to draw up his own outline, although this should be kept simple.

It is helpful to notice that the Gospel is easily divided into two distinct parts. Chapters 1 to 12 are concerned almost entirely with our Lord's public ministry while chapters 13 - 21 deal with his private ministry to his disciples, except for chapters 18 and 19 which record His trial, crucifixion and burial. The reason why chapter 21 has been designated as an appendix is because the Gospel as we have it in its earliest form may well have ended at chapter 20. This is generally accepted among biblical scholars. A careful reading of chapter 20:30-1 and a comparison with chapter 21:24-5, both of which are editorial comments, will help us to see how this may well have been so. Such a theory in no way encroaches upon the inspirational value of the book as a whole. The author of the first twenty chapters is certainly the author of the last.

ANALYSIS OF THE GOSPEL OF JOHN

CHRIST'S PUBLIC MINISTRY

Chapter	Verses	Content	Place
1:	1-14	Prologue	
	15-36	John the Baptist heralds Jesus	Judea
	37-42	Call of Andrew and Peter	Judea
	43-51	Call of Philip and Nathaniel	Galilee
2:	1-11	First Sign: Water into Wine	Galilee
	12-25	Cleansing the Temple	Jerusalem
3:	1-21	Nicodemus	Jerusalem
	22-36	John the Baptist exalts Jesus	Judea
4:	1-42	Woman of Samaria	Galilee
	(31-8)	The Fields are already for harvest	
	43-54	Second Sign: Nobleman's Son	Galilee
5:	1-18	Third Sign: Healing the Paralytic	Jerusalem
	19-47	Judgement and Eternal Life	
6:	1-15	Fourth Sign: Feeding the 5,000	Galilee
	16-21	Fifth Sign: Walking on the Water	Galilee
	22-71	The Bread of Life	Galilee
7:	1-52	They seek to kill Jesus; and Words of Eternal Life	Galilee
8:	1-11	Woman taken in Adultery	Jerusalem
	12-59	The Light of the World	Jerusalem

9:	1-41	Sixth Sign: The Man born Blind	Jerusalem
10:	1-42	The Good Shepherd	Jerusalem
11:	1-44	Seventh Sign: Raising of Lazarus	Bethany
	45-57	They plot to kill Jesus, who retires to	Ephraim
12:	1- 8	Mary anoints Jesus	Bethany
	9-50	Triumphal Entry: Jesus speaks of his death	Jerusalem

CHRIST'S PRIVATE MINISTRY TO HIS DISCIPLES

13:	1-14	Washing the disciples feet	Upper Room
	15-38	Jesus tells of his betrayal and gives a new commandment	
14:	1-31	I am the Way, the Truth and the Life; Love one another: Jesus promises the Holy Spirit	Upper Room
15:	1-27	I am the True Vine Keep my Commandments	Upper Room
16:	1-15	Jesus Promises the Holy Spirit He speaks of his departure	Upper Room
17:	1-17	Our Lord's High Priestly Praye	Upper Room

TRIAL, CRUCIFIXION AND RESURRECTION

18:	1-11	In the Garden	Jerusalem
	12-18	Peter's denial	
	19-27	Before Annas	
	28-40	Before Pilate	
19:	1-16	The scourging	Jerusalem
	17-22	Jesus is Crucified	
	23-30	He gives up his Spirit	
	31-42	The Burial	
20:	1-18	Jesus appears to Mary Magdalene	Jerusalem
	19-25	Jesus appears to his disciples, not Thomas	
	26-29	Jesus appears to his disciples, with Thomas	
	30-31	Ascription by the writer explaining the purpose of the Gospel	
21:	1-14	Jesus appears to some of his Disciples by the Sea of Galilee	Galilee
	15-25	Our Lord's commission to Peter	

BIBLIOGRAPHY

Author	Title	Publisher
G.R. Beasley Murray	John	W B C
Wm Barclay	The Gospel of John	St A Press
C.K. Barrett	The Gospel according to John: An introduction with commentary on the greek text	S P C K
F.F. Bruce	The Gospel of John	P & I
D.A. Carson	The Gospel according to John	I V P
C.H. Dodd	Historical traditions of the Fourth Gospel	C U P
C.H. Dodd	The interpretation of the Fourth Gospel	C U P
J.D.G. Dunn	Baptism in the Holy Spirit	S C M
M. Green	I believe in the Holy Spirit	H & S
W. Hendrikson	Exposition of the Gospel of John	Baker
M. Henry	Commentary on the Bible	M M & S
A. M. Hunter	According to John	S C M
G. Hutcheson	John	B of Truth

139

R.H. Lightfoot	John's Gospel	O U P
J. Marsh	The Gospel of St John	Penguin
Leon Morris	New Testament Theology	Academia
Leon Morris	The Goospel according to St John	Eardman
J. Packer	Evangelism and the sovreignty of God	I V F
J.C. Ryle	Expository thoughts on John	H & S
S. Smalley	John, evangelist & teacher	Paternoster
G. Smeaton	The Holy Spirit	B of Truth
R.V.G. Tasker	The Gospel according to St John	Tyndale P
W. Temple	Readings in St John's Gospel	Macmillan
B.F. Westcott	The Gospel according to St. John with greek text	J Murray